750

LIFE AND TEACHING OF THE MASTERS OF THE FAR EAST

By Baird T. Spalding

Volume V

 DEVORSS *Publications*

Volume 5
ISBN: 0-87516-367-X

5 Volume Set
ISBN: 0-87516-538-9

DeVorss & Company, Publisher
P.O. Box 550
Marina del Rey, CA 90294

Printed in the United States of America

EDITOR'S NOTE

Baird T. Spalding played a very important part in introducing to the Western world the knowledge that there are many Masters or Elder Brothers who are assisting and guiding the destinies of mankind and the earth.

The books, LIFE & TEACHING OF THE MASTERS OF THE FAR EAST, have been used and sold by many lecturers and teachers of Truth during the past thirty years, in order that the knowledge contained therein might be broadcast to all corners of the earth. These channels were used by the Elder Brothers for the specific purpose of educating mankind that it might become aware of and turn its attention to these Great Laws of Life; for, as Jesus said: "The things that I do ye too shall do, and still greater things shall ye do."

TABLE OF CONTENTS

THE LIFE AND TEACHING
OF THE
MASTERS OF THE FAR EAST

by Baird T. Spalding

Baird T. Spalding, whose name became legend in metaphysical and truth circles during the first half of the 20th century, played an important part in introducing to the Western world the knowledge that there are Masters, or Elder Brothers, who are assisting and guiding the destiny of mankind. The countless numbers of letters that have come in through the years, from all over the world, bear testimony of the tremendous help received from the message in these books.

Partial listing of the contents of the five volumes:

Volume I: Introduction of the Master Emil—Visit to the "Temple of Silence"—Astral projection—Walking on Water—Visit to the Healing Temple—Emil talks about America—The Snowmen of the Himalayas—New Light on the teachings of Jesus.

Volume II: Visit to the Temple of the Great Tau Cross—Visit with the Master Jesus—Jesus discusses the nature of hell; the nature of God—The Mystery of thought vibrations—Jesus feeds the multitude—An account of a healing experience—Jesus and Buddha visit the group.

Volume III: One of the masters speaks of the Christ consciousness—The nature of cosmic energy—The creation of the planets and the worlds—The trip to Lhasa—Visit at the Temple Pora-tat-sanga—Explaining the mystery of levitation—A doubter becomes convinced of the existence of Jesus.

Volume IV: This material was first presented as "The India Tour Lessons." Each chapter has text for study, as well as guides to teachers for developing and interpreting the material. Among subjects covered: The White Brotherhood—The One Mind—Basis of coming social reorganization—Prana.

Volume V: Material taken from lectures given by Mr. Spalding in California during the last two years of his life. There is also a brief biographical sketch. Partial contents: Camera of past events—Is there a God—The divine pattern—The reality—Mastery over death—The law of supply.

Each of the 5 volumes has approximately 175 pages.

PUBLISHER'S NOTE

Both Mr. Spalding and Mr. DeVorss (who knew Mr. Spalding personally) died in the 1950's. The people who were associated with Mr. Spalding on the tour have also passed on. We are therefore without contact with anyone who has firsthand knowledge of the work, and the books themselves are now the only source of information. To our knowledge, there is no map available of the tour, and we know of no photographs. We have tried at various times to locate additional records, as well as camera information, but without success. We sincerely regret that we have no additional information to offer.

DeVorss & Company

BAIRD T. SPALDING

BIOGRAPHICAL SKETCH

WHEREVER there is a flare of general interest in any personality or his achievement, such as has been evinced by the readers of THE LIFE AND TEACHING OF THE MASTERS OF THE FAR EAST, you may be certain there is a flame of spiritual Truth accompanying it.

Few in modern times have created such an interest as Baird T. Spalding, whose name became legend in metaphysical and Truth circles during the first half of the twentieth century. Few sensed the flame of spiritual inspiration sweeping the world as did Mr. Spalding. The nature of the man, the manner in which his message has been presented, and the Message all bear living testimony to the Truth of his words and the honor and sincerity of the man.

The countless numbers of letters received through the years from all over the world bear testimony of the tremendous assistance from the message contained in his books and such letters continue to pour in, years after he passed over to a higher schoolroom.

Baird T. Spalding passed beyond the veil on March 18, 1953, in Tempe, Arizona, at the age of 95. He was active in his mining interests right up to the end.

Douglas K. DeVorss probably knew Mr. Spalding as well as anyone, due to their many years of association, and we quote from his talk given at the Spalding Memorial Service in Tempe, Arizona, on March 22, 1953:

"Mr. Spalding was a very quiet, humble servant of all whom he met. He would never permit me, under any circumstances, in presenting him to audiences, to dwell on the personality or on himself as a man of great accomplishments. Since 1935 I had the unique opportunity of traveling with him to more than 200 cities in North America. And, though I lived with him 24 hours a day in a very close relationship most of those years, yet I must be frank and tell you that I do not believe any one person or group of persons really understood this great soul, for so many different ways, on so many different planes of activity. In making these few personal remarks, I am sure you understand we are doing this in a very humble way, because not only was he our friend but a man who was like a father to many of us.

"There was not a town of any size anywhere in the world, that I know of, where Mr. Spalding couldn't walk into someone's home and sit down to dinner. He was always welcome. And during the past twenty-five years he lived very much, as we say, like a bird. He seemed to have reached a point of attainment where material things were not of great concern to him. Although his earnings as an individual, over a period of time, were unknown to me and to all of us, nevertheless, he passed on not as a rich man at all. His material possessions are few. The great heritage which he left is in the unique discoveries which he made regarding the teachings of Jesus. Mr. Spalding never wrote or lectured for financial profit or gain and he was an open channel for any funds that came to him, distributing them immediately. We have no way of knowing the extent of his philanthropic enterprises because no one ever approached him who was in need of any material assistance that he didn't give them everything he had and, consequently, he was always a very prosperous man. In fact, I know of no one who, in a way, was as rich as Mr. Spalding and many of us envied his unique attainment which he had reached through his very exceptional understanding, and which undoubtedly came to him very early in life.

"It was about 65 years ago that he first made some of these discoveries regarding Jesus and the lives of the Great Masters. He walked and talked with Great Masters in the visible world, even as did the great scientist, Mr. Steinmetz, of whom he was a great admirer. I have seen pictures of Mr. Spalding and Mr. Steinmetz together. Both Steinmetz and Edison predicted that the time would come when it would be possible for us to make recordings of the Sermon on the Mount and in the actual language and voice of Jesus at the time when He gave the Sermon on the Mount.

"Many other startling discoveries and disclosures, as I like to refer to them, were made by Mr. Spalding during his long life of service and activity in all parts of the world. For instance, I want to go back to the idea of how his books came to be published. I have been told by people who knew Mr. Spalding in Calcutta, India in the early nineties that he decided to write out in longhand some of the accounts of his experiences in India. Some friends asked him to type it and let them have copies, and for many, many years he carried these typewritten accounts (of what later became Volume I) with him. People would read them and pass them among themselves until, finally, a very prominent woman in Oakland, California, whose husband was the builder of the Oakland Municipal Railways, asked Mr. Spalding if he would have any objection to her having her printer, the California Press in San Francisco, print a thousand copies of this work in an inexpensive paper binding; she wanted to give every one of her friends a copy of that book. Mr. Spalding gave his consent and soon after this he left for England.

"The books were printed and passed among her friends, as a gift. Within about sixty days, phenomenally, as it seemed, more than 20,000 orders were received for copies of that book! When Mr. Spalding returned from England, of course he was astonished at the interest in his discoveries and experiences, so he permitted her to have the balance of the work published, which became known as Volume II.

"Then there was a period of about ten years that Mr. Spalding did not do any writing. But nearly every night he was a guest or visiting friends and after dinner he would have a little question and answer period and in that way he met a great many people. After his day's work was done as a research engineer, he would answer the many questions put to him at these little gatherings and the word-of-mouth publicity spread very rapidly. But that work came to a halt during the period when Cecil B. De Mille was making the moving picture, the KING OF KINGS. Mr. Spalding was engaged by Mr. De Mille as technical advisor on all the Biblical work in that picture.

"My experience with Mr. Spalding started about twenty-five years ago. I was particularly interested in the books and their distribution throughout the world. At that time there was a great upward surge in New Thought and spiritual reading and studying and many people were very anxious to have Mr. Spalding complete another book. Finally, one of his very closest friends invited him to a country cabin where he could work without interruption and Mr. Spalding completed in longhand what is now known as Volume III. That book was published immediately.

"A rumor started spreading across the country that Mr. Spalding had passed on, so I suggested to Mr. Spalding that, since he was not sailing for India and a trip around the world until October 4, that we go to New York together, stopping at some of the larger cities enroute, and meet the many people who had been reading his books and disprove the false rumors being generated. Mr. Spalding agreed that this would be a good idea if it would be accomplished in about thirty days. So, the latter part of August, 1935, we selected thirty of the larger cities and decided to make that tour in thirty days. I have a reason for telling this because, as many of you know, Mr. Spalding, right up until just a few days ago, had almost unlimited energy in a physical form.

He was never fatigued. He could go for maybe two or three weeks with only three or four hours sleep a night.

"He never claimed anything for himself. He never made any claims as to being a great healer or practitioner, seer, psychic, or anything of the sort. And I can assure you he did all of his writings just as you sit down and write a letter to someone. The material was never obtained through automatic writing, clairaudience or clairvoyance, or anything of that sort. It wasn't necessary because he knew these people whom he wrote about just as he knew these great scientists and religionists, such as Dr. Steinmetz and Dr. Norwood. The latter was the famous clergyman in New York and one of Mr. Spaldings's very close friends.

"I think these facts may be of interest to you, although he probably wouldn't approve some things we are doing here this afternoon because he realized that the physical form had so very little to do with the real Life of the individual. As you will recall, he said: 'The Christ is in each one of you,' and that is the important thing that he wanted everyone to realize. Sometimes when people asked him, 'How many Masters are there in the United States?' he would say: 'There must be at least 150 million Masters in this country.' That was the vision which he had, that each individual would become aware of his Oneness with God and the Christ and not just worship creeds and dogmas and sects.

"Each one of you, as individuals, if you were standing here in my place, could tell a little different story. No two stories would be alike as to what Mr. Spalding meant to you as an individual, as a brother, but through the writings and his talks, answering your questions, he never put any limitation on time. I have known him to talk all night to a friend to help him over some mental or financial stumbling block. It was almost as if he had some great intuitive power that made him such a great scientist. He had studied in Heidelberg. He had worked in all the great scientific laboratories at one time or another, particularly in geophysical work. He was one of the early pioneers in the atomic work. He was particularly interested in helping the individual to help himself. Strange today, and the most difficult thing for people to understand, is that material possessions seemed to mean so very little to him. Because he realized, as Jesus did, the greatest thing that we can do when we are expressing on the physical plane, here on this earth, is to live the Christ Life and get our attention away from limitations. Of course, that is what we have tried to do this afternoon because we know that Mr. Spalding is with us as always and that we have the continued opportunity of living the Life as he did and in the way which he tried to show us."

FOREWORD

The following chapters are taken from lectures delivered by Mr. Spalding in Southern California during the last two years of his life.

CHAPTER I

CAMERA OF PAST EVENTS

FROM the shadow of the Himalayas to the great vastness of the Gobi Desert; from New York to Central and South America; from San Francisco to the Philippines, Alaska, and Canada, come these experiences, findings and revelations of our research work.

We have been carrying on this work for over forty years, first translating the records which we found in the Gobi, in Tibet, and in India, and this work has developed into an organization of about twenty-six men who are interested in and doing the work.

The scientists are beginning to give us a great deal of credit; in fact, two years ago they believed that, with our new camera and what we call taking pictures of past events, we are going to be able to go back at least one million years, showing the civilization that did exist at that time.

Now that may seem rather remarkable, that we can go back and take absolute pictures of what happened thousands and thousands of years ago. There is a great deal being done along that line. We have the distinction of starting it because of Dr. Steinmetz' assistance. I worked with Dr. Steinmetz myself and, during that whole time that I was with him, he put forth the expression, "We'll build a camera that will go into the past and pick up every past event, if you wish it." He went on and delineated. Not only that, he drew the plans for that camera and we followed through and today we can say definitely that we can go into the past and pick up every past event. Of course, that becomes too cumbersome, but we select past events and, as I said, the scientists are admitting today and fully believing that we will go into the past events to the extent of a million years.

Our initial experience with the first camera was motivated by Dr. Steinmetz. I worked with Dr. Steinmetz for about nine years, and he always maintained that we would eventually go back into past events and could get everything that happened, in fact, show what civilizations did, how they operated, and so on, and that has come to pass.

Our first experience was with George Washington's inaugural address. That was in New York City at what is now known as Federal Hall. In that picture you can readily discern every one of the dignitaries who were on the platform with him and George Washington is walking back and forth before the group giving his inaugural address. At that time there wasn't even a still picture taken of that address or that group. Paintings were made but no actual photographs. Now we have the actual picture, with George Washington's voice on the sound track. Everyone said for a time that it was a fake because they claimed that we made it up in moving picture form. But it can now be shown with a regular moving picture mechanism.

Then we went from that to the Sermon on the Mount. Now we know that Jesus, the man, was no different than we are. We have a complete history of that family's life for over 20,000 years, and know that it was a well established family, that He was a man of great influence, a very definite character. He was a man six feet two and, standing in a crowd, you yourself would select Him and say, "There is a man who will accomplish," and He *did* accomplish. History is bearing those things out today and we are going back to this drama and getting the absolute words.

We are very much interested in His whole life and we followed it through at great length. Not only that but we have known the man for a number of years and we know today that He never passed through death.

Now Jesus of Nazareth never claimed for himself any more than what the ordinary person was capable of doing. That we know for certain. Not only that, He told us that death was overcome.

The Sermon on the Mount has lived on and on as a spiritual masterpiece. People regard it as such today, more than ever before, and they are beginning to understand it and take it into their lives.

We can show you in photography today that no one brought anything except the little boy with the five loaves and fishes. This isn't an allegory. If it were, we wouldn't find the boy there in that picture. Neither would we find the people there. All Jesus said was, "Sit down and prepare for the feast," and there was an abundance for all.

19

Then again we have the instance where the disciple said to Jesus: "Master, there is need for bread, yet it is four months to the harvest." His answer was: "Look upon the fields, they are already white to harvest," and they are, right in the picture.

With those pictures we have been able to correct many mistakes that have been made. We worked for eight years on the picture, the Sermon on the Mount, before we got the identity of the man, Jesus. We were always looking for a man of the description that da Vinci had painted.

We had an interesting experience in this connection. Three of us were in the Vatican and we were talking with a very elderly cardinal who asked us how we were getting along with the picture "The Sermon on the Mount." He was quite interested in what we were doing and told us that we would get a lot of information if we would take his card and go to the Louvre in Paris and ask for a certain man and ask to see daVinci's letters. This was a new lead for us and we were on our way to Paris immediately. We went directly to the Louvre upon arrival, where every courtesy was shown us. Leonardo daVinci's letters are all there today and this can be proved.

We have always felt that daVinci's painting was a portrayal of Jesus as he saw Him. It has been proved today, and we have daVinci's letters proving this, that he saw the Christ in the face of the model he chose to sit for the portrait. He said the man was young, engaged to be married, and there was a beautiful light in his eyes. DaVinci interpreted it as the Christ and painted the portrait as such. This was during the renaissance period when long hair and the beard were the custom. We have never known Jesus to wear long hair and a beard, and in robes. Maybe other people have but there it is written out in daVinci's own hand.

Two years later the artist decided to paint a picture of Judas, the betrayer. He searched for nearly two years, looking for one he felt was despicable enough to portray the betrayer. Finally, one morning he was walking through the apache quarter in Paris and here, in a little niche, all dishevelled and in rags and down and out, was the man! He walked up to him and said: "I have painted a portrait of the Christ, now I am looking for a man who will pose for me for the portrait of Judas, the betrayer." The man looked up and said: "Sir, I posed for the Christ for you." It was exactly the same man! DaVinci goes right on to describe in his letters how, had that man never betrayed the Christ, he never would have found him in the niche in the apache quarter in Paris. He even goes so far as to say that when we use the word "can't" we deny the Christ within.

Today we can prove that every negative word that you use, you betray the Christ within yourself. Now daVinci went right on to say that he never thought of portraying the countenance of Jesus, the Christ, but he did see the Christ in that face.

Leonardo daVinci was a most remarkable man. He wrote many scientific articles that are very fine, yet they have never been published. You can only read them by going into a glass cage with three men watching you while you read them. They are very valuable. He was a very exceptional man and he spoke of the Christ within all the time. He explains how wonderful it is to represent the Christ, to *see* the Christ in every face. When he was painting in the Vatican and the cardinals found him asleep on the scaffold and they called his attention to it, he said, "While I am asleep I am doing more work than while I am awake." While sleeping he saw everything right before him that he would paint and in the exact colors he would bring out, and he would get up and put them down. He said, "Everything that I see is an exact resemblance and the vibrations of that which I put on the walls are the vibrations that I pick up, and I can manifest those and bring them forth with perfect ease after I see them in my sleep."

QUESTIONS AND ANSWERS

How do you select the events of the past?

A. They are all in a certain band of frequency. Everything that you say, your voice and words, goes right into a band of vibratory frequency and it goes on and on.

Q. What is the best path to pursue to obtain illumination?

A. The path is right within. Search ever deeper within yourself. *Know* that this great Light belongs to you. That is all that is necessary.

Q. Were you born in India?

A. Yes, I was born in India and my father was born there too. I attended preparatory school and later Calcutta University. Dr. Vose and his wife at that time had been there for 68 years.

Q. Did Jesus and the disciples and other Bible characters really live in the flesh as we know it?

A. Oh, yes. We have a number of their lives through the camera of past events.

Q. What did Jesus look like when you saw him?

A. He is a man six feet two. If He were in this group tonight you would recognize Him for what He is, a man of the greatest attainment, just as He looked upon everybody, with the power to attain everything, and He did, and He always has. He is living today just the same as He always did. We photographed Him exactly the same as we might photograph you. We have pictures of Him walking arm-in-arm with Luther Burbank, with Doctor Norwood, and a number of others.

Q. Are all of these great problems that afflict the minds of men completely overcome when we live the life of the Masters?

A. Yes. Jesus' firm statement was that the Truth makes you free.

Q. How does man get rid of the idea of man not being God?

A. By refusing to accept the negative statement. The statement: "I Am God," frees you from the negative statement that you are not God. It is better to state the Truth than the untruth.

Q. If you make the statement, "I Am God," and are unable to accept your unity, is it not a matter of blind faith?

A. If you make it wholly on blind faith you have made a separation and will fall short of the goal. It is far better to say, "I can," and then go right on to "I Am." If you accept the "I can't" attitude you have accepted a separation from God.

Q. If man is God and God is Spirit, where did the material body originate?

A. As an hypnotic influence in the mind of man. It has no basis in fact. Man brought the material into existence. The mortal body is an hypnotic body and when man wakes from that state it will be to him as a nightmare. He wakes to dream no more.

CHAPTER II

KNOW THYSELF

FRIENDS, we are going to take up here what has been shown and proved in over sixty years of research work. We have the scientific proof today that every function, every thing in this whole universe is Divine. Name that Divinity what you will, the greatest name is the word "God." Why? We can show you today that that word vibrates at the rate of one hundred and eighty-six billion beats a second and we know people capable of intoning that word. But the beauty of it is, the moment that you realize that vibration, you *are* that vibration every time.

Now it is established in every form. It isn't just your form or the form of anybody else; it is established in everything and, were it not for that divinity, we are proving today that we couldn't take a photograph. There wouldn't be a form in this room that we could photograph today if it were not for that divinity.

Now we have absolute proof of that. Then why say that I am not divine? You just leave the "not" out of that and see what difference it will make. *I Am* divine! And there's the truth about yourself. The untruth is—I am not divine. The truth is, *I Am* divine. Complete the saying and carry right through — *"God I Am."*

We make those statements for the very reason that we *know* today. You have been told that, yes, but what someone else tells you, you may take with a grain of salt or you may say, "Well, perhaps that person doesn't know," but today we *know* through experiment in photography and high magnification and we can take any person and ask him to sit before this camera under high magnification and it will show that divinity every time.

Our bodies started from the one cell and the multiplication of that cell built this body. And we can show, through high magnification today, that that light never ceases. It is transmitted from one cell to the other as this body is built up. It doesn't matter what you think about it or what you say about it, it is established in that vibratory frequency and it never goes out of that frequency.

There is proof of these things today. The eye, one of the greatest things in our body today, is also adjusted; the rods and cones and the retina are so adjusted that they take in that divinity, the moment that we realize that divinity our eye becomes adjusted to it and the frequency that it moves forth at, and it can be shown that those who have not in any way impaired their sight, that they themselves see that almost immediately by the acceptance that they are divine.

Now divinity is God in everything, in every form. The Christ means the power to realize that divinity within. Then don't we see the Christ in every face, in every form? That was one of the very first statements that Jesus made. We find that in our research work.

"I see the Christ in every face, in every form. When the first child was born the Christ was born."

That is the conquering Christ, the one that conquers, the Master of everything. There isn't a person today but what is the master. Now the moment you say that, people begin to look for a master. The moment you look without for the master you forget all about the master within, and humanity has made the greatest mistake by looking for God or trying to see God. Why? Because you are looking for that which is right within you and when you pronounce that you *are* that, you *are*, every time. We can show you that if you will use the word "God" once, in standing before that high magnification, your body will never go back to the same frequency in vibration that it was before you used that one word.

Another thing, we can show that the word "God" is so established in a book that that book has a greater eminence because of the presence of that word. We have three men who can intone that word to one hundred and eighty-six billion vibrations a second. We asked them to go to the 180th parallel, which is the farthest you can get away from Greenwich on this planet. Then, at a certain stated time, we arranged this instrument so that it recorded the vibration that they intoned. Just as soon as that frequency came in, the hand went right up to that point. Now we put the oldest Bible in the Museum of Natural History in London under that instrument. Then we gradually removed that book and slipped in a book in which the word "God" was not recorded and the instrument went right back. Then we took a third book in which the word "God" was recorded only three times and the instrument responded immediately. Just one word, "God," was responsible for this response in frequency. If it will do that to an inanimate thing, what will it do to our body form by the positive use and acceptance of the word "God."

With the voices of three men intoning the word "God" at one hundred and eighty-six billion vibrations a second, the graph goes across a thirty foot film. Then, with these same men using the word "Jehovah" it marks only about five inches on that same film. Why? The moment that you use the word "God" with understanding, and belief, and knowing, you are setting up the greatest vibration that is known today, and that vibratory influence collects substance, and the moment that you put out your thoughts, a condensation of that substance is yours and, in fact, to put it forth in the right order, you can't keep those things from you. Now that is what belongs to everyone — every good thing that they can use. You set up that vibratory influence and it manifests here and now.

There is a very definite principle that we are working on today, that principle of divinity in everything. This has been proved by our camera taking photographs of past events. We can show that every blade of grass, every tree, every shrub, every flower, every seed is divine and, were it not for that divinity, that seed would not grow, nor the plant, nor the tree, and we can show you definite photography today that that germ in that seed has the exact replica of the form that it will bring forth every time. Then why do we go about saying we don't understand? Isn't it greater to say, "I do understand"? You *do* understand! That understanding is right within yourself. You are the master of those things and, by letting go of outer appearances, you master the thing within, accepting and recognizing that you *are* the master!

Many people write and ask if they cannot go to see the Masters or what must they do to see the Masters. The moment you step out from yourself with your thought that you wish to see a Master, you have lost sight of the Master within. When you recognize and become aware of that, you are *with* the Master and you are with all of Them.

Now just let someone say, "I am not God," then stop for a moment and take that "not" out. That is a negative word and has no frequency in vibration whatever. You give it the energy that keeps it living by pronouncing it and the moment you refuse to pronounce that word it has no energy of its own.

There is a camera that shows you that today. You can actually sit before that camera and make your statement, don't say a word but think it, and we will give you your exact thoughts from the graph shown on the film. Then we ask for a statement with a negative word, just to see what happens, and when it comes to that negative word there is no graph on the film. It simply is not recorded.

That camera is showing today the great frequency of vibration of the human form and, if that frequency was not there, we would not get it; and, if there were any hypnosis used, it would not record.

We have taken over four or five hundred pictures

of the fakirs of India and, wherever hypnosis is used, the camera doesn't get it at all. We have had two or three very remarkable instances among those hundreds of pictures taken. On one occasion we were returning to our home in India and when we arrived there was a man standing just inside the gate. He had placed an orange seed in the ground, put his little mantilla over it, and it was coming up. He removed the mantilla and the orange tree came right on up and in forty-five minutes apparently there was a tree there, the branches, the buds, the flowers, the leaves, and then the ripe oranges. We were taking pictures of that. There were twelve cameras in the group, and we ourselves were so deceived at that time that we stepped up and attempted to pick oranges off the tree, and the tree wasn't there!

One of the men developed two of those films and I kept the young fakir in conversation until they returned with the two films. I unrolled one before him and said, "How come? You fooled us but you didn't fool the box." He was quite perturbed over it and said, "Tomorrow you come, I show you." It was agreed we would meet on the following day at eleven o'clock.

The next day we were all on hand at the appointed hour; and we had exchanged cameras. On this occasion the young fakir brought with him a man whom none of us had ever met before. He came forward willingly, put the seed in the ground; our group was taking pictures all the while. The tree came up in identically the same way. We all saw it. This time we wouldn't attempt to go up and try to pick oranges off the tree, we had been so badly deceived the day before. Finally the Chief said to us, "Well, what's the use? If it isn't there, then let's find it out." He walked up and picked an orange off the tree and ate it and each one of us did likewise. That tree is still bearing oranges on our place in India!

Here is what happened. The young fakir was the chela of the old guru. When we explained to the guru what had happened the day before, he became quite irritated and dismissed the chela and refused to have anything more to do with him. He told us that they carry their chelas through all of the twelve methods of hypnotic influence to show them that there is no existence there, that nothing is accomplished there, but if we will let go of them all and *be* this, then everything we do comes forward.

It comes under the art or law of suggestion, and we have studied it in India. For example, we see a man come out with a rope in his hand. A small group who are curious gather around him and he throws the rope up in the air, apparently, and then calls a boy out of the group to climb the rope. Maybe the boy disappears at the top of the rope, and that is all that is necessary. The man collects a few coins, enough to give him a living for a few days. Now we have taken pictures in 500 instances of those exhibits, and the camera gets nothing on the film but the man standing there before the group. There is your power of suggestion. It is brought out so definitely that you stand there and believe it.

The old guru is working with us today over in India. We take a seed, plant it in the ground, irrigate the soil mechanically, and in seven minutes we have a stalk of corn with two ears fully developed. This old guru, when he puts a seed of corn in the ground, before he raises up, the plant stands before him! He has no mechanical devices at all. He just *knows*. Now there is the best evidence in the world that we ourselves are perfectly capable of that accomplishment. It belongs to everybody. If anyone ever accomplished those things, then all have the privilege. No one is selected, each has the ability within himself. There is nothing complicated, in fact, it is very simple, and we need no lessons. It is merely bringing one to the point where he sees or is aware of the advantage of accepting those things, and then giving thanks that they *are*.

This power is present and works in everything, in our daily living, even in the money that we use. There is no need of anyone being in want. There is no want, in fact. We simply fail in our expression, and we call it lack. Now let go of another "fail." There is no failure!

Many of our medical scientists today are saying that in the future man will live a hundred years longer than he does today. Age is simply a state of consciousness and when man learns to let go of old age he will go on and on. A year makes no difference in our thought structure until we say that one year has passed. Then we immediately qualify it with one year older, whereas if we would think of it as a year of greater accomplishment and achievement, a year of greater illumination and understanding, it would be just that.

The greatest thing that we can do is to *see* the divinity in every face, in every form. Our greatest privilege is to see the Christ in every face and that means the unlimited power to *know* God within.

We can go right back to all of those things and prove them today. We don't ask you to take them on hearsay. You can prove it for yourself by letting go of old age, of limitation, and all negative thoughts, refusing to use them or accept them in your world.

We know historically that about 3,000 years ago one language that was spoken did not have a negative word in it, and that language goes back for over 200,000 years.

QUESTIONS AND ANSWERS

Q. Does the word "God" spoken silently have as much power as the word spoken audibly?

A. There is just as much power. In fact, to many people it is more powerful to think "God" within than to speak it.

Q. How can we set in motion this great power within for self-expression?

A. Simply by *knowing* that that power is yours. You are the Supreme Power. You are the Supreme Wisdom and, the moment that you accept that, you set the energy free which shows you that you are free from any limitation whatsoever.

Q. Will there be great destruction on this planet before there is universal peace?

A. The destruction is what we put on ourselves. The thoughts that we put out. Now, supposing we all refused to use the word "destruction," would there be any? Not at all.

Q. What holds back the knowledge of the great Masters from readily spreading throughout the world?

A. It is our own fault, nothing else can hold us back. The moment we *accept* and *know* that we are as They are, and always have been, why it will never be held back at all. Nobody can hold it back from us but ourselves.

Q. Is hypnotism trespassing the law of subjugating a man's will?

A. Hypnotism has been generally conceded to be a very detrimental thing to use on the human form or human brain.

CHAPTER III

IS THERE A GOD?

IS THERE a God? We have that question asked more often than any other question today.

Science has given a great deal of attention and thought in recent years to this subject and is really doing a magnificent work in research along this line. The research was suggested by a group of medical scientists and it has been in progress for several years now.

Of course, there is a very great determination that there is a great Principle back of all experiences. This goes back so far that all continuity of it has been lost through the ages. We are coming to realize that it has always existed and does exist today and nothing can move that Principle out of absolute law and order.

The greatest question humanity has asked and is still asking, is: "Is there a God?" From an orthodox point of view it is accepted on faith that there is a God, a divinity called the Father of man. In this way we are speaking for a great division of humanity. Yet, in no way satisfied with believing on faith alone, they ask to know: "Have you irrefutable proof of the existence of Divinity?"

It has been the task of science to investigate the matter and find the answer to the question, an answer which will satisfy the rational mind.

Through scientific investigation in recent years it has been discovered that there is a Universal Force, which is also termed Universal Energy, a primal energy, pervading the entire universe and filling infinite space. Today we are finding that the energy that that Principle manifests is greater than the atomic bomb. That energy emanates throughout all space, all conditions, and all things. It is not given just to one person or to one group, it is all-in-all and it belongs to everyone. It works with everybody, whether we realize it or not. The non-realization of it makes no difference whatever. It is not concealed under books or in dark places. It is ever-present, omnipresent, pervading all things. It is the very substance and principle from which we live and move and have our being. Were it not for that very Principle, that Divinity in every person, we would not be able to take a picture of this group. Experience has proved this. This Divine Principle has residence within and permeates everything, every method of life and experience. It is that Divine influence, that Divine Energy which is permanent, everlasting, all-encompassing. We have proved that through photography, for were it not for that Divine Energy, no photograph could be taken. The pictures recorded on a film are simply the emanating vibrations coming from the object or person of whom the picture is taken.

This is proof of the Divinity within each form. If we seek that Divinity from without, we fail to find it, for we are looking outside ourselves for that which is as near to us as our hands and feet, as close to us as our heart, right within us. If we will go within, we will find Divinity in all phases. Then why waste our time searching without for God?

It is the same with the Masters, or Elder Brothers. They are right here, within every form. They are as near to us as our heart. You do not have to travel to India or to any other country to see these Masters. You can see them right where you are. "When the student is ready the Master will appear."

It is well known today that through a greater civilization, many, many ages past, a great reservoir, as it is called, was built up of the principles and God-qualities and attributes that have been generated and manifested through countless eons of time, and that reservoir of good cannot be invaded by any condition of the negative whatsoever. The mighty reservoir or momentum of God-good energy and pristine purity stands there for all time and the instant we think of that great vibrating, pulsating principle we become aware of it right within ourselves. That vast reservoir of good stands ready and waiting for our use at all times. We have but to tune into it, to become at one with it.

Now that energy has been called by the name "God," the word that is receptive to the greatest vibratory influence known today.

When we use that word in its right meaning, and it can be used in no other way to have any influence, we act upon all substance; we act upon every principle; we act upon all law and order, and that which we pronounce in good form is already ours. Just as Jesus said: "Before ye have asked I have answered, and while ye are yet speaking I have heard." Think of it! Because we have sent forth in definite order and definite form, the Word, at that instant that which we state belongs to us! There is no time or space.

It is well known today that perfection never could be created. It always *was* and *is*. If we think through our expressions to create perfection we go outside of ourselves completely, because perfection is already created and is here and now; therefore, by using right words, right thoughts, right actions, every word impinges upon that great vibratory influence. The thought first and then the word expressed.

In our Bible it says: "In the beginning was the Word, and the Word was with God and the Word was God."

As we learn to throw out every negative thought, feeling, word, and action, we conserve that energy within our own form. The moment we speak a negative word we are dissipating God's pure and perfect energy; therefore, the more we learn to discipline ourselves to think, feel, speak, and act positively and constructively, the more of this potent energy do we generate to fulfill our calls and manifest perfection.

Every statement made by Jesus manifested here and now. In His world there was no future, all was *now*. In the original language there is no word for the future, there is no word for the past. Every word in that language is the expression of here and now. In like manner it is known today that every word we speak under positive, constructive influence is recorded and it never goes out of existence.

The very definite statement, "I Am God," is a determining factor in carrying humanity onward. With that ideal we progress.

Each individual may prove this statement for himself. It is the one who can project an ideal, and then hold his vision true to it, who accomplishes, in many cases unconscious of how he has done so.

Worship is not an idle action. It is necessary to put forth an effort to realize the ideal. That ideal held completely in thought must come forth in form. The thought in itself brings the thing into visible form. That vision projects so definitely that it is called from the source of all being and consolidated in its entirety. A clearly presented vision precedes it.

It is important to hold to one condition at a time. Never permit your thoughts to wander at random or even to project another form until the first one has been accomplished. After the action is completed, let the thought go completely and turn to the next action.

This is the definite understanding which Jesus had. "Ye are Gods, and sons of the Most High." That was His thought regarding the fact of human existence. Always the highest; always the noblest; always the purest; always Light. Never anything that might limit life and energy. Never failing, never doubting. Always the same singleness of purpose directing thought. This projected vision can carry humanity above any fear or discordant condition of thought, can keep humanity always at that level of high accomplishment, going from a lesser to a greater field of usefulness.

Such is the progression of our planetary system. The suns of all solar systems express in that way, drawing energy to themselves that greater energy may be given out. If our sun were a great lump of coal, it would sometime be consumed. No, it has existed for hundreds of millions of years. It draws to itself force, power, energy, making it available to our world as well as others. Man must learn the same lesson of the exchange of energy.

The moment we withhold our forces, stagnation takes place. But, if we give forth of what we have, the new always flows in to refill the space left by what was given out. The energy is inexhaustible if we use it in the right way and in the right direction. That is why this body of ours is renewed. If that energy is without us, it is also within us.

If divinity is without, then we cannot keep it from within. All that one need do is to make of himself a channel for the divine force. It is always pulsating and cannot be depleted. This is the essential explanation of man's immortality. There is an immortality to every thought, every act, and every word. There is a coalescing force which man cannot escape. What man generates and emanates accomplishes the fact which has always existed. The fact of all being has always existed in spirit without beginning or end.

Man always questions the nature of beginning. It is not easy to conceive of anything without an origin. As far as man is concerned, beginning came into being with conscious or separate identity. Before that, man was spirit, and that state is one to which we shall return.

The new attitude toward science and religion will enable us to realize the better things which have been promised. They are here now when we shall have opened ourselves to receive them.

God is in no way the form of a human being. God is that Supreme Intelligent Power that permeates every form and every atom of the whole universe. When you realize that Supreme Intelligent Power is fully centralized within your form, you are that Power, and by fully acknowledging that this power acts through you, you are that power. Each and every individual has the ability to *be* that Power. This is the God Kingdom into which every individual is born and, as soon as all see and *know* this, all are of God's Kingdom.

QUESTIONS AND ANSWERS

Q. What is the first law?

A. The first law is I Am. That is the lost word. We are beginning to realize it. God I Am.

Q. I should like to know more about the "I AM" as the Masters presented it to you.

A. "I Am" is the second word in the language. It means the complete acceptance that you are God. God I Am. The word "God" is the first, because of its greatest vibration, and then your acceptance is "I Am."

Q. What is the Holy Ghost?

A. The Holy Ghost means the whole of the I Am spirit in complete action in every form.

Q. How does one bring forth the Christ?

A. The Christ must be born within each one. Jesus gave us the example of this. You bring forth that which is within you by turning your attention to and concentrating upon that very thing. The Christ is within you.

Q. If these Masters you write about are able to leave their bodies, how is it that so few people know about it?

46

A. Because the people don't believe it! They do not leave the body, that is an expression which is used so that it can be understood. They take their bodies with them.

Q. Have you ever contacted Saint Germain?

A. We know of Saint Germain and know of his life. It was a great life. No one knows that Saint Germain ever went through death. My adopted brother and I had an interesting experience in this connection. He was engaged in a great government engineering project in this country. After he left that, Paris cabled him to come over there. They had under advisement the draining of a great swamp back of the City of Paris and making it a fertile country for gardens. As they proceeded with that, the Seine began to encroach upon Saint Germain's tomb and they realized they would have to move it. He cabled me and suggested I come over, as they would probably open the casket and we could view the remains. I went over. The casket was opened and in the casket was found only the thigh bone of a dog! Now think of the thousands of healings that went on in that place. They put all of their thoughts upon the accomplishment of Saint Germain, they lost all track of their infirmities, and complete perfection took place. Now that is so with nearly every one of the shrines today.

Q. When we wish something that is ours by divine right, is it right to demand it?

A. If anything is yours by divine right, there will be no need to demand it. Our own acceptance of illusions negates the good that we want. When you give expression to the divine nature within you, you will find whatever you will use at hand. The realization of this permits you to know that the good is accomplished before you express the thought. The need does not have to arise.

CHAPTER IV

LIFE ETERNAL

FROM a select amoeba the Divine Image never changes. It dominates the ideal and perfect form and passes on that perfect form unchanged to every new cell that is created in the entire form. Thus every cell of the bodies of the entire human race not only *has* the perfect but *is* the perfect image of Supreme Intelligence. Thus we have the unassailable proof that man or humanity is the divine, supreme intelligence, which is God, the Conquering Christ, God-man, the result of the complete coalition of the Trinity. Indeed, every seed has the exact image of that which it will produce.

Now let us sit quietly and look directly at this select amoeba and its ability to reproduce and send forth and unerringly implant its perfect image into every cell that, through multiplication, forms not only the human form but every tree, every blade of grass, every flower, every crystal, and every rock, as well as every grain of sand. In fact, by the close examination of crystals, all rock structure can readily be classified. It is thus with every grain of sand as well as with all minerals. This crystalization is the foundation from which we learn their relationship to the whole and their relationship and economic value to humanity.

Let us return again to the high magnification and rapid photography which is being developed. We find that the minutest seed, when its germ cell is photographed under high magnification, has the exact form of that which it will produce and bring forth unerringly, and it is giving off a wave length or a vibratory frequency which accompanies it through-out its circle of productivity. And through its frequency of vibration it attracts to itself the energy that is necessary for its development into maturity; and this frequency of vibration, which is the divine life essence which accumulates or draws to itself the substance, not only gives life to the tree, the flower, and all vegetable life, as well as all minerals and metallic substance but it is the very life of that substance.

Now we are free to say that all substance has life expressing through it. And there is no change from that divine plan of perfection until man, through his thoughts, either enhances or debauches the perfection. It is also found that man is able to influence these emanations of perfection to a larger and greater productivity of presenting greater and greater thoughts of productivity and more abundant perfection.

Let us return again to the amoeba or first cell. While this cell is entirely different from that of the vegetable or mineral, its rate of vibration is much greater and is not to be compared with that of the mineral or the animal. It is found that its rate of vibration is the force that draws its energy or substance to itself, which causes its growth into new cells, which finally builds a human form, and the passing on to every cell created the first perfect and undeviating form of divinity. It now can definitely be seen that when humanity cooperates and in no way, through thought or expression, interferes with the ideal of divinity, the human form is ideally perfect. Thus we can say that it is God-body, pure and perfect.

Let us see that divine energy and intelligent principle emanating from the single cell or amoeba, which its own principle of great vibratory frequency began drawing energy to itself and then began dividing and multiplying until it came into a great focal point or form, wherein it could emanate and direct all forms as well as put forth forms as of the image of itself. Humanity has never deviated from that perfect pattern or image. Photography shows those perfect forms, not only surrounding every form, but also other perfect forms coming forth.

Where the scientists lack evidence, we have forged ahead to the complete *knowing* that we are that great emanating frequency. Sit quietly for a few moments with the statements, *"God I Am, as all are," "God I Am Divine Intelligence,"* and know, and then admit to yourself, with all doubt removed, *"I Am Divine Principle, I Am Divine Love, and it flows through me to all the world."* Then see yourself as God and everyone you meet or see, as God, and you will see that which is being accomplished in the sub-microscopic zone of life, for you will see an almost invisible drop of protoplasm that is transparent, jelly-like, capable of motion, drawing energy from the sun. It is already capable of using the light of the sun to break up the carbon dioxide in the air, forcing the atoms apart, seizing the hydrogen from the water and producing carbohydrates, thus making its own food out of one of the world's most stubborn chemical compounds.

This single cell, this transparent droplet, holds within itself the germ of all life. It not only has the germ but it has the power to distribute this life to all living things, great and small, and it also fits that creature to its environment wherever life exists, even from the bottom of the ocean to the universe above. Time and environment have moulded the form of every living thing so that it meets the infinite variety of all conditions, and as these living things develop their individuality, they sacrifice some of their flexibility to change and become specialized and fixed, losing the power to go back but gaining a better and greater adjustment to the conditions as they exist.

The power of this droplet of protoplasm and its contents is greater than the vegetation that clothes the earth in green, greater than all of the animals that breathe the breath of life, for all life comes from it and without it no living thing would have been or could be.

You will find that all of this is absolute Truth, step by step. Humanity will know, as we know, that man is the universal source of this life. Man is master in the animal as well as in the vegetable and mineral kingdoms, completely endowed with Supreme Intelligence; in reality, the soul of all things. This Divine Intelligence man has never lost. He has only become shamefully unaware of this true God heritage through the setting up of his own debased thought structure. It is well at this point to stop and let go of, forget and forgive this debased thought structure, and set up a real structure as man, the Supreme Intelligence, the master of all things; God and man, one.

An amoeba is a microscopic highly developed living cell composed of untold millions of atoms in orderly arrangement. Size is nothing to the Infinite. The atom is as perfect as the solar system. This cell divides and forms two. The two divide and form four, and so on, ad infinitum, as cells do in every living creature. Each cell contains within itself the power to produce a complete individual. The cells themselves are immortal. They form the cells of all creatures, animal and vegetable of today, and are exact replicas of their progenitors. We, as all humanity, are well-ordered replicas of billions on billions of similar cells, each cell a citizen intelligently doing its full quota of devoted service. This one cell also has the power to use sunlight to break up a chemical compound and make its own food and enough for its brother cell. You will find that this division is absolutely basic as one of the essentials of life itself. Can it be further denied that man is immortal here, when there is every proof of divinity as immortality?

All things that live start from a single cell and this cell compels all of its descendants to perform the service and follow without deviation the design of the creature the original cell is to duplicate, whether it be a human, a turtle, or a rabbit. It is found that these cells have distinct intelligence, instinct as well as reasoning power, as it is well known that after division, portions of these cells are forced to change an entire nature to meet the requirements of that being of which they are a part. Why? Because the plan is set forth and is invincible to change and that is the reason that man is divine, perfect, and invincible. It does not matter what thinking structure he evolves, this plan is absolutely irresistible and can never be changed; it is first principle, dominant and compelling, and is also the very reason that man is capable and abundantly able to reach the highest. In the event he fails to reach the highest in his immediate understandings, all that is necessary is for him to change his thought structure, which has circumvented him, to the true thought structure that is steadfastly fixed within his own mind, of which he always has an inherent instinct, and build a dominant thought structure which will allow him to reach to the highest conception to which thoughts can aspire. His easiest and most successful way of attainment to this highest goal is forever to let go or drop the thought structure that has bound him to the wheel of repetition and set into immediate action that which will build up an invincible thought structure which will never fail in carrying him to the highest.

The first suggestion is to place in his mind the thought and word, "GOD," knowing positively that it is the one point from which and where all success originates, also from which all success emanates.

Then fix that thought of success with the thought, *"God I Am success."*

Then the next thought, *"God I Am abundantly able to succeed in every effort that I truthfully designate."*

Your next statement will be, *"God I Am the exact knowledge that goes with the ability to succeed."*

Your next statement will be, *"God I Am the infinite love that attracts all substance to me that brings forth my success."*

Knowing also that love is the greatest cohesive power in the universe, your next statement will be:

"God I Am the intelligence that guides all of my success into right and profitable channels."

This will be followed by:

"God I Am the divine knowledge and the wisdom that gives the perfect to all of my success," followed with:

"God I Am the perfect trinity, God the Conquering Christ, God-Man, the one focal point of all creation."

We are now dealing with God cells which never lose or change in any way, thus man cannot change from Divinity. The brain of man is built of these God cells and this is the very reason that mind never changes. Thoughts may change one thousand times a minute, as they are only reflexes from the subconscious. It is there that man has free will, for he can induce the subconscious to believe and store any thought put forth or that which he perceives or is told by another. This subconscious is no portion of the brain itself but it is a ganglia of true cells located just below the heart center. These cells know neither impurity nor imperfection. They accept and store everything that is thought or spoken and they have no way of discriminating. They also repeat that which they have stored and man soon begins to believe what is repeated as truth. Soon he is unable to segregate truth from falsehood. This group of cells, however, may be influenced to let go of all false statements or falsehoods and accept and register true and absolute statements simply by talking directly to them. Suggest that they let go of all false and negative qualities, thoughts, and statements and you will soon be aware that only true and constructive statements are registered in your world, which in turn reflects to you and through you. Then will follow the awareness of a great serenity of purpose. These cells have no way of discriminating except as they are taught. You will find that they are very tractable and most willing to be led or influenced by the truth. Many people have seemed actually to bound forth in response to this application of truth.

Hundreds of billions of cells are impelled to do the right thing at the right time and in the right place and, verily, they are obedient at all times as long as the individual is sincere.

The life of man pushes forward building, repairing, extending, and creating the new and better with an irresistible urge and energy that is not comprehended by or found in inanimate things. It is found that there is an intelligent instinct and directing influence that pervades every cell of the human form, it does not matter how far they may seem to have wandered from this Divine Directing influence. It is our privilege to see them in this influence without giving any thought to the outer or that which is holding them under the hypnotic spell. What a privilege it is just to see that one or all who are under the spell really endowed with that infinitely complex cellular structure called the human brain. That same brain has the capacity to carry man or all humanity to the very highest of attainments. What a divine privilege it is to see all humanity combined in this great structure of God Mind.

Try this "I Am of the noble God Mind" and see it open the windows of heaven and let it pour out such a blessing that it fills completely every avenue of expression. All those who are faithful need say— *"God I Am the knowing principle of all things."* This opens the eye to the universal abundance that never fails. Try it, knowing positively that you must succeed. As Elijah did, hold out the cup until it is filled to running over. Never doubt the capacity of the One Mind. It is always ready to bring forth these wonders, as humanity aligns itself with God Mind.

As such, humanity has been traced with sufficient evidence to satisfy scientists, for at least one million years but let us see that this period is but an established minimum, for man goes back to an antiquity far beyond all human understanding. You can readily see that you are capable of extending your vision with the inclusion of God Mind, or the One Mind, to furnish all humanity with a background or build-up that has maintained true to man and Divine Mind; and how readily you are able to attach your thinking process to Divine Mind by declaring—*God I Am Divine Mind*—then knowing definitely that your statement is true and in full accord with Divine Law and Principle.

In this way you are fully aware that heaven is all around you. Now is the opportune time to know that all are as free to accomplish this as you are. Now realize that matter was never conceived until thought set it up as a reality. Remember that matter never smiles, neither does it have any power or energy to rule or master itself; it is also devoid of instinct or volition of its own. It is foreign to all other substance.

The bird actually sees its destination of migration and thus does not need an instrument to guide it; that instrument is right within those tiny brain cells. How much greater can the same instrument guide you, for it is right within your brain cells, and mind is in direct control as soon as man knows that he is in full control of mind action. The bird, although it flies over a thousand miles of open water, never loses its direction.

Man has this same sense of seeing but he has lost the ability by putting it out of his thought structure. Nothing is ever lost from Divine Mind. This is the very reason that it belongs to man, for man is as divine as mind. Thus he will never deviate from truth or be at a loss to accomplish all things when he again joins with Divine Mind.

The animal has never lost instinct and intuition for the very reason that it is incapable of building an adverse thought structure. When a dog is set upon the trail of man or beast, he is incapable of thinking,

"Can I do this?", consequently he goes forward and follows that trail until something happens that obliterates the scent or the goal is reached.

Man is far more capable than the animals or the birds, yet he permits himself to sink lower than the animal.

With the true perception of man's fully equipped make-up and his full understanding of his complete inclusion within God or Divine Mind, man is readily capable of moving from position to position with unbounded velocity, his brain is now fully equipped with True Mind and, as he cooperates with True Mind as all-seeing and all-knowing, he scales every height instantly and perfectly; there are no wanderings, the path is clear, the evidence is revealed with certainty and sureness.

You can put out your hand and feel God. Put your hand on your own form and you both see and feel God. As you may have passed 100 or 1000 people during the day in going about your affairs, you have seen God 100 or 1000 times. This may be repeated each day. Keep God close to you by seeing every living form as God. Then God will be so close to you that you will never again closet God in some far off celestial realm or temple and you will find the temple not made with hands. You will also find that your body is the first and greatest temple ever built and that it is the only temple wherein God abides. Then see the Conquering Christ and God-man within this temple. This is the very life that maintains your body. Take God away or separate one from the other and your body would die.

Man has built all of the great temples that have ever existed or do exist upon the earth but he has never duplicated this great body temple. It is not only the greatest laboratory ever built, it also has the power of duplicating itself.

Man has defiled this body temple to the utmost, even to the place where he is obliged to lay it down in so-called death. Yet it rises again triumphant!

Man, under limitation, is unable to build a human eye but let man throw off every limitation and he is able to build or renew an eye or any part of the human body even to overcoming death.

There is a divine intelligence and principle but it was never set up by one being or one man. It was set up by a great civilization of hundreds of millions of people. This thought was set up so dynamically that it saturated every atom of the entire universe as well as every atom of the human body; also, with a directing influence upon all things. It was also set up with such power that it became a directing force of mind action, where nothing changes. Thus it impressed its power upon every cell of the human form and the light which denotes this divine intelligence was centered in the first cell to the extent that divinity has been passed on from generation to generation for billions of years, without a change in the real Divine Image of each unit of humanity. It will go on unchanged for a hundred billion years, as it is established as Immutable Law, and an established law in the cosmos is unchangeable. Law should be Lord, as there is but one law, one Lord for all established mind action. Man is the Lord in full control of divine law.

Out of this great action came millions of years of peace and thorough contentment. Each one was the conquering Christ-King of his own domain, yet a willing helper and worker, with no thought of self or selfish ends in that which was the good for all, as an abundance of all things were there for all to use.

Then groups claiming free will of thought and action began withdrawing unto themselves. They longed for a change; they wanted to know of material things and to think of themselves rather than for the entire group. Thus larger numbers withdrew from the main household, as it was called at that time. Finally the groups of dissenters combined and grew to the extent that their thoughts became chaotic, until the natural elements were thrown into chaos and a great eruption took place within the sun, which lasted for at least a million years.

At different intervals have come the planets and stars of our solar universe. Yet prior to this chaotic condition humanity had already set up in definite mind action such a divine balance that to chaos has come order so divinely exact and perfect that the place any star or planet will occupy at any time can be mathematically determined to the second. This balance is so perfect that there has been no variation for a billion years. This certainly indicates eternity. Thus you can readily recognize perfect law, or lord in action, and it came into being through a great civilization of the human family and through their united will of perfect understanding through the civilization.

To this divine understanding was given the word or name GOD. It was fully known that this word could be intoned at the greatest vibratory frequency, as it was placed at the head of all language. In the beginning the word in no way represented a human form but it did represent a great Divine Principle set up by the entire human race. This race lived in heaven, as heaven to them was and is the ever Divine Principle and harmony within the human form, which is the mind called God. From this word, knowing its divine origin and precepts, every divine condition does come to humanity. This divine, just, and perfect law, or lord, reigns throughout the entire universe. You now see it throughout the entire solar system but we know that it is just as positive throughout the entire human kingdom as well as in the plant, mineral, and animal kingdoms.

During this chaotic disturbance nearly all of those who had withdrawn from the great group were destroyed. Those who were left of this group were obliged to seek shelter in caves and wherever they could find protection. Food became scarce, and just the matter of food became so pressing that a large percentage became cannibals. These conditions, which they brought upon themselves and which not only separated them from the great group but from each other, forced them to form tribes in order to exist, thereby causing them to forget all of their former knowledge, and so they became nomads.

These were the forefathers of that race which is

called "material." And although this separation has carried on for well over a million years, there still remains something which may be called a half instinct through which they feel that they have been a part of the divine plan. Many of these are fearlessly coming forth today and freely proclaiming their Lordship and a portion have advanced to the point where they are entirely free from all bondage.

Those who did stand together in the great group went through all of these chaotic changes in perfect peace and composure without any loss of divinity, as they knew that divinity could never be lost or taken from them. For all this they are in no way claiming any selectivity, neither do they claim any power above that which all can use.

During the period that this great civilization reigned upon this earth the great land areas, as well as the seas, were peaceful. There were no land or sea disturbances, the breezes were gentle and invigorating, and all of the people traveled at will wherever they wished, as there was no weight or cumbrances, no limitation of time or space. They thought in terms of eternity. All thoughts and words were put forth as divine precepts and to such a definite purpose that they were firmly fixed and definitely recorded as precepts in divine mind, and these were the foundation and bulwark of a great reservoir that could be drawn upon for every supply, every action, and every undertaking. Thus man had at hand a universal supply for every undertaking and every accomplishment. For all humanity was looked upon as God-man and the Trinity, or completion, or focal point was God, the Conquering Christ, God-man, the Trinity complete in all.

There was not a negative word in the language, neither was there a word for a past or a word for the future; all was here and now and completely accomplished and finished. All of the accomplishments that humanity is struggling with today in order to return to this high estate have been accomplished by this so-called higher civilization, and all of the accomplishments are recorded in record form and are accessible to humanity as soon as they will look beyond this so-called material age with its welter of divided precepts and personal accomplishments. All of these accomplishments are perfected and fully recorded definitely in the great storehouse of universal mind substance. They can be called forth by mankind as soon as they still the clamor of those who through their own free will forged the calamity. The greatest hope is for the future generation. It is quite evident that the younger generation is physically, mentally, as well as mechanically the best of all timber; all that is lacking is courtesy and judgment tempered by experience. These qualities will bestow maturity. The greatest substitute and guide is habit, for a good habit is as easy to acquire and as difficult to break as a bad one.

It is a well organized thought by those who are the survivors of that great civilization, that had every individual been carried out by these great chaotic disturbances, that the precepts were so definitely thought out and so thoroughly recorded in the universal mind substance that not one thing would have been lost. It is a well known fact that every positive word set forth with a true meaning and definite intent is so fully and intelligently recorded in Divine Mind substance, which we call God Mind, including every action and tone, that it can be recalled, also photographic records made to the degree that all may see and hear all of these events.

It is a well known fact that a portion of this great civilization has survived and preserved their identity. Although they have withdrawn into more or less seclusion, nevertheless they are awaiting the time, which is not far distant, when they may come forth and proclaim their identity. It is now stated that this time will be when a sufficient number have let go of their preconceived ideas of a personal God or great being outside of themselves and accepted the Trinity, God, the Conquering Christ, God-man in all, and capable of being set forth through and by all mankind.

These records can in no way be varied or distorted, neither can so-called time distort them. These are no miracles or super-human experiences; they are natural, fixed conditions. In fact, they are of the same fixed law that governs and rules all of the planetary systems of the universe. The wonder is that this law and its influences speak more loudly than any words the greatness of man's ability to achieve. The great beauty and purity of it all is that this was in no way a great dominating or supernatural race; just as you and I are today all in the same image and likeness, the same and one God. Then let us all worship together this one great noble God-Man, looking first for God in all, then seeing the Conquering Christ in every face, uniting all in God-man; knowing that every image that is set up outside of man is but an idol with feet of clay that is readily broken by the spoken word. With this you can clothe all science and all religion with the same garment from the one source, as all is one truth. Truth is the law of all science. By thinking divinity man establishes divinity within himself and also adds to the great reservoir of cosmic energy and force, that force becoming a great power within itself. You are capable of setting up just such a force and building it to a higher degree of activity. There are millions adding to that force all of the time and you can join them if you will.

QUESTIONS AND ANSWERS

Q. Where do inspirational ideas come from?

A. The world of ideas is all about us. You may have any one of several conceptions regarding the meaning of inspirational ideas. Most so-called inspirational ideas are emotional expressions that have little significance other than that of deep feeling. Other inspirational ideas are those flashes of clear-sightedness that enable one to act wisely in an emergency. Possibly the questioner has in mind that profundity of thought achieved by philosophers and saints by means of their disciplines. This is the real, consciously breathing in the spirit of universal wisdom that permeates all space.

Q. How do we get inspirational ideas?

A. In a sense we generate them within ourselves by disciplining our bodies to serve as channels to receive the currents of universal mind and transform the one force in such a way as to intercept the universal laws that are expressed in the diversity of phenomena.

Q. Why do our ideas seem to come from outside sources?

A. At our present stage of development we are not prepared to recognize the source of all the forces that are active within us. Life is a universal force which we know in living tissue but we do not know where life comes from or where it goes when it leaves the body. Electricity is used every day; we know it may be generated but we do not know where it comes from. To describe thought as a force expressed in ideas that are generated may be somewhat less tangible but the analogy is evident. We think but the source of the energy is hidden; yet we do know that we can increase our thinking capacity and efficiency. Is it any wonder, then, that the average mind is confused when it is said that thoughts come from within? It certainly does seem that they would have to come from without; but so it is with electricity and life. Prepare certain conditions and life and electro-motive power are at your disposal. Prepare the mind and inspirational ideas will be generated within you just as surely.

Q. What is your attitude toward the present upsetting social conditions?

A. I do not give them any energy. If we would withdraw the energy we give to thinking about upsetting conditions and build up our own bodily conditions with that energy instead, we could correct any conditions immediately.

CHAPTER V

THE DIVINE PATTERN

I AM GOING to take up the subject of what one person can and does accomplish in this thought. Our experiences in this connection were very considerable at the time of our expeditions into Tibet and India, also in Mongolia, and we observed the ability one has to protect not only himself but an entire race.

That may seem like a tremendous undertaking but, when we go back and think of Jesus' life and realize what He did for humanity and what He is doing today, we are better able to comprehend and accept it. His teachings have never ceased for 2,000 years. They have gone on and on and they are just as vital today as they were then.

I have told of the Masters standing on the water and the two students who walked out to them. There is a great lesson in that demonstration. It shows how we can control and use natural forces and benefit by them, not necessarily walking on water, but as we get out of the objective state, where we see we are going to sink, and move into the subjective state, we can use that power to assist this body completely. In that state we accomplish. There we are not subject to change. The change is only the changing object. The subject never changes. Spirit is never in any way altered. The basic principle always maintains.

69

Now if we look always to that basic Principle we become that Principle. Some may think it would carry us into a static condition. How could it? It is in that very attitude that we become able to accomplish and then we go on without change but with an accomplishment along a definite line, knowing exactly what we are accomplishing, not just what we are going to accomplish.

If we live with that one attitude of thought always subject to our understanding we cannot change. There is always progression. That carries us right on into another statement or condition, and that is old age.

Old age is objective. We accomplish that ourselves. But is it necessary? Not at all. Suppose that we could travel into space a sufficient distance so that we were completely away from this earth. There is no time there. Supposing we stay there for one hundred years as we count time. We would be no older. The same condition can be brought directly to the earth. In fact it really is here — no time and no space — conditions subject to our determination. Medical scientists are telling us that there is not a body in existence over nine months of age. We are subject to the change that we put upon it only. Youth belongs to us. If there were not that perfect condition, we would never present youth at all. If youth is not always eminent, there would be nothing youthful. If youth were not subject to our will, we would all be old.

Now we make old age subject to our will. A child

is born. Its elders see three score years and ten for that child. The child becomes subject to the thoughts of the elders. We do not even give that child a chance to fashion its own future. We fasten the idea of death upon that child. The Hindu says that three score years and ten is the time when man reaches his majority, when he begins to accomplish. From then on he can go on as far as he will with no limitation, with youth completely subject to his determination.

It is said that we make a success of everything we undertake. If it is failure we undertake, we make a success of that. If it is perfection we undertake, we make a success of that. How much better it is to present perfection than imperfection. If we did no more than assist our neighbor, it would be much better than to present imperfection to him. We would get much more out of life and it wouldn't cost us a penny. It costs nothing to greet him with a smile. Present love to him and perfection will follow right along the same line.

Think of an assemblage joining with just that one object in view: youth, beauty, purity, and perfection! Is it going to cost us anything to live by those ideals? If we would live with those ideals always foremost, we would change our conditions within a week's time. We have seen it accomplished within a moment.

Didn't Jesus say that "If your eye be single your whole body is full of Light?" It is impossible today to take the originals of Jesus' teachings and find where

71

He put anything into the future. He gave man the greatest scope to use his thoughts to one definite end and that end is accomplishment.

We have seen a single man able to accomplish a condition where nothing could touch him. He was not a so-called master, either. He was a Sioux Indian and it happened right in this country. We know of conditions among the Indians today where they can draw a line around their villages across which no one can come with hate in his heart. It was attempted twice and in both instances the attempt proved disastrous.

Jesus said: "As ye love one another you are immersed in love." He placed love as one of the greatest powers. When we turn our power in the other direction we come into a state of turmoil. He said that you are the ruler of heaven and earth and all that is in them. Are there any limitations in that? He saw that man had not touched his possibilities. He presented the unlimited to humanity.

If there were one atom misplaced in the body, that body could not remain in existence. Take one atom out of place and the whole universe would explode. Jesus presented those conditions in a simple, straightforward way. His original words are perfectly simple. He placed the ideal so definitely that we could never forget it. He presented it as "God." It is known today that the vibratory influence of that word carries us right out of the hypnotic state we build in our own bodies. If we turned the energy we give to that state toward God, we would build that condition so definitely that there would be no separation.

But most of us look from the central point and allow our thoughts to dissipate. Jesus' vision went to one point, that subjective condition that always exists. The object changes but the truth never changes. Now if we changed and gave all our energy to that one-pointed attitude, our bodies would emanate light. When we came into a room that room would light up. We have seen that many times. It is not phenomena. It can be photographed and you cannot photograph phenomena. We can turn from the unstable condition, in which we have chosen to live, to the stable condition and it takes us only as long as it requires us to take the thought. The very instant we have changed our thought to this Truth, or God, it is right with us and we are that very thing.

We do not need any lessons. Lessons only make us aware. They are a power, yes, but we are apt to give more energy to the lesson than to the meaning it conveys. It took only one demonstration for those two students to walk out and stand with the teachers on the water while the others stood on the bank. There are many standing on the bank because they do not change to a stable condition. The same amount of energy they give to instability would take them right out on the water. We do not need to leave here to learn to walk on the water. Nor do we need to leave here to learn one single precept. There is but one precept, and it is right here within us. We cannot change it. It does not matter how long we keep away from it. When you turn toward the light, you find that you are the light. Did Jesus need to walk toward the light? Why, He *was* the Light. It is, as He explained, the light of truth, the light of love, the Light of God.

Jesus never used a thought that was not turned toward principle. With that attitude we can all follow in that very simple way. Those people who live in that simple way do not take something from someone else but bring out from within. That is worked out to the supplying of food and every necessity. The only difference between them and the rest of mankind is that they have projected their vision to take in a wider horizon. Everyone can work it out for himself. Once we have worked it out we have learned the rule. We follow our own course and then we *know*. Paths may be presented and ways shown but unless we use our own way we are not going to accomplish it. If we look to others, we are adding energy and impetus to something that someone else is doing and we are giving that energy from our body. The moment we present our way we add energy to our body and we have ample to spare. That builds up a condition that helps everyone. We do not take the thoughts of another to build upon. We build our thoughts into universal condition that benefits the whole of humanity.

It is said that no one brings forth an accomplishment in any way without assisting the whole race. It is the energy we add, directed toward one great attitude of thought, that carries humanity on. It is not by building upon the other fellow but by building upon our own foundation. Then we have all the energy in the universe to use.

Everything we think of in the name of God, and

74

with that vibration, belongs to us. That covers all supply, all knowledge, all purity, all perfection, all good.

You can gain dominion just as soon as you put your entire thought on the fact that Divinity is already established within you. Know all of the time that Divinity is nowhere but right within; that it has always been established within; that you have only clouded and thus kept it out of your consciousness by your own adverse thoughts.

Talk to that Divinity within. Tell It that you know that It is there and that you have now become fully aware of Its presence. Ask It to come forth and be the dominating factor in your life. Say, *"I now have let go and now put out of my life all adverse thoughts. I Am grateful that Divinity is fully established throughout my entire being."* Determine that you will no longer be an animal, that your entire body is now so pure that the Holy Presence of the living God has attained full possession of this body temple, and that It is now in complete charge. Keep these thoughts constantly in mind.

Then say, *"I now know the bliss and satisfaction that spring from the union of the soul with the Living Christ and that bliss and satisfaction do abide in me throughout all eternity. I know that the Presence of the Living Christ is fully established in me and I Am the pristine purity of the Christ."* Keep these statements before the subconscious or subjective mind and you will soon experience the joy and satisfaction that always have been yours through the Presence of the Living Christ.

Soon you will find that you do generate mental forces that supplant all adverse thoughts, feelings, and actions. You do build up a momentum of pure thought that is irresistible and that dominates your entire world. The time to fortify this spiritual and Holy Temple is when we are at peace with our own soul. In this way we so educate the subjective mind that it gives forth nothing but Divine impressions. This sinks deep into our consciousness and operates during every hour of our sleep. When we find a weak spot in our thoughts, words, or deeds, it is necessary to bring the will into full action to strengthen and fortify these rents in the structure. Soon we learn automatically to conquer all adverse thoughts and only God-thoughts and God-feelings have residence in our worlds. Then do we truly have the armies of our thoughts and feelings so marshalled that nothing but God is able to enter. This is the degree of absolute Mastery, where one attains the ability to make the Divine Principle manifest. Thus we are the basis of all Spiritual Power. You will find that it pays great dividends as you make it your work in life. You now see the dawn of a new day and you do gain a greater understanding of the Law.

There is no more effective way to free your mind and world of discord than positively to *know* that your entire mind and body is the Temple of the Living God. You can also use this statement with the knowledge that, through the silent but far-reaching influence of Divine thoughts, all humanity, in fact, the entire universe is benefited and raised by every constructive thought, feeling, and spoken word sent out by you. The more you think of the immortal Love of God, the greater the enlightenment of humanity manifests. Thus you can see and understand, in a measure, the tremendous privilege and opportunity which is ours in assisting in the uplifting and enlightenment of mankind. What is more, it is our responsibility and our obligation to life to help erase or dissolve the negative in the world of humanity, and one of the most powerful ways to do this is by refusing to see, hear, or accept the negative, and consciously to send forth Divine Love to everyone and everything. Know firmly that *"The Divine Spirit of the Conquering Christ transcends all discord."*

Know always that your will is the Divine Will, God's Will, and that God is acting through you every moment! Each thought that you qualify with this master thought increases your will power and your will power becomes so strong that your very thought is irresistible. Do this and expect results with all sincerity and nothing can disturb you.

The persistent, daily use of such strong, positive words and thoughts, repeated with great intensity, develops dormant brain cells and you soon know that you are the Lord in full dominion. Exercise your will and your word for all purposes and you become the master of your own mind and no longer accept the negative qualities in the world around you. As you are faithful over a few things you become master over all things. Create, through your word, the condition that is rightfully yours and you are the master over all conditions.

Physiologists now state that the cells comprising

the organism of our bodies have the power to receive impressions and carry them to the complete cellular structure of the human form; also, the power to recall impressions, or memory, the power to compare impressions, or judgment, and the power to select between good impressions and imperfect impressions. It is also well determined that the subjective or subconscious mind is the aggregate energy and intelligence of all of the body cells. By putting forth only Divine impressions, all of the cells again become aware of the Divinity of each cell, and they transmit this Divinity to every cell of the human form. Were this not true, no photograph could be taken of the human form.

As this becomes known to the individual, the will force of each individual cell agrees and works in harmony with the will of the organ or center to which it belongs and to which it will attach itself. It is the power of all of the will cells composing the organ or center and it is brought into conscious harmony with the central will of the entire organism of the human body. Then as we use the words, "God I Am," it is fully manifest through the entire body form. It also gives greater power to the next spoken word, such as *"I Am God Power, I Am all Abundance,"* and so on, and *"Through this Word of Power I Am free from all limitation!"*

QUESTIONS AND ANSWERS

Q. Will you explain what you mean by God?

A. God is the principle by which we abide. You cannot put a definition on God. The moment you begin to define It, It is above that definition. A definition only attempts to crowd God into the quart jar of man's intellect.

Q. Some use the word God, some Spirit, some Principle. Which is best?

A. The greatest word is God. You cannot set up a hypnotic condition with the word. With others you can. If you turn directly to the one point, there is the greatest accomplishment. You cannot utter the word "God" too often.

Q. You speak of Jesus seeing the golden-white light. Is that the highest attitude?

A. We do not know. It was far above anything of an objective nature. Nothing of a lower potentiality can penetrate it.

Q. What method should be used to contact Divine Power?

A. There is no set formula. As we look upon it, the law is where we are, always. If we definitely put ourselves in tune with the law, the whole universe opens to us. If the universe is open to us and we see every condition of the universe, we are manifesting under this law and we become one with it. It is done simply by *knowing* that we are one with it, never allowing any doubt or fear to enter.

Q. Is the western world prepared to accept these things?

A. The western world is preparing and the preparation is going on so rapidly that no one is excluded. People only exclude themselves. We create the field when we open our understanding. That field can be expanded to take in the whole universe. The universe of our body is one with the universal whole at all times and it is only for us to expand our understanding to become one with the universal whole.

Q. How shall we discriminate as to what thoughts to project?

A. If we are not able to discriminate, we should give out Love to the best of our ability and refuse to give out anything else. That will bring us to harmonious conclusions. Jesus placed Love before everything else.

Q. How does it happen that every so often an Avatar is sent to earth?

A. The presentation of Principle is what you would call the selection of an Avatar. That person merely lives close to Principle. The path which he shows, or the life he lives, becomes the path for all.

Q. Is his appearance and reappearance dependent upon any condition of spiritual unfoldment on the earth?

A. No, he steps through all unfoldment and lives one with Spirit.

CHAPTER VI

"KNOW THAT YOU KNOW"

I HAVE BEEN asked to give out a statement of healing.

In reality, we only heal ourselves. There is a very potent factor there, because the moment that you see the Divinity, or God, within the individual, you and God are the majority, always. Now God, or that Divine Principle, knows nothing about imperfection. We know today that is exactly what transpires at the healing shrines throughout the world. In going to those shrines the people put their thoughts wholly upon the accomplishment and fulfillment of perfect health, accepting the emanation that the shrine represents, and the healing takes place.

We can show you that in photography. A very fine doctor in one of our large cities worked with us. He asked his associates to send him cases with certain conditions that could not be healed by medical fraternities, together with their x-rays and records.

The camera used shows where the diseased portions of the body are. Where life and health maintain, the film shows the body radiating, scintillating with light. We had patients under that camera whose light went out from the body for thirty feet! Not one person in the 98 cases worked with ever remained before that camera three minutes before they were completely healed and walked away.

All we did was to say, "Here, you are paying all of your attention to the dark spots, aren't you? You are not paying any attention to the light and these light places and where the light is coming from. Now just let go of those dark spots completely. Put your whole thought and attention on the light!" Every one of the 98 cases, each of whom was brought in on a stretcher, walked away completely well! Now isn't that evidence that you heal yourself? You treat yourself and that is absolute.

If we would adhere to these positive expressions, we would soon see that there would be no more disease. It has been named a certain disease and we keep repeating that name over and over. Now thoughts and names are things and, if we will put them forth in the absolute position in which they were intended and in the vibratory frequency in which they belong, perfection will manifest. That is true in the case of every invention that has ever come forth. A great many of us think we have to get in and dig and dig.

We discovered that in our research work. We had no logarithms to go by. We built them up ourselves as necessary. We would get so far and then find we had made a mistake and go back and work it over again. We are like little children learning to walk; but today we are able to walk because we have the mechanical devices and we are building more devices today that will take up from where we leave off.

Here is an experience we had, to make my point: We needed a man for a specific work. We had been working for a long time on a given problem and were seemingly at the crossroads, when this young man came up from Columbia University. He had never had any experience with this type of work, yet in twenty-five minutes he had solved our problem! Here we had been working on the whole thing for almost four years.

Now what happened? He *knew* that he *knew* every moment of the time and he went into that office and he said to himself: "I know this situation," and he brought forth the solution, just by *knowing*.

I have had the same thing happen and I know it is real. This happened to me at Calcutta University. I joined what is known there as the preparatory school for Calcutta University when I was four years old. The very first day I attended, the teacher said to me: "Here is the alphabet, what do you think about that?" I said, "I don't know," and he replied, "Well, if you keep that up you never will know. Now turn right around and let go of that 'I don't know' and *know that you know* what that is," and through that very thing I went through that school and went on and completed Calcutta University when I was fourteen years old.

These things are so simple we pass them up. We think when we go to the university that we have to get in and dig and dig; dig it all out of books. Anything that has ever been written in a book is already known. If you will take that position, you will know it too. You make a book a crutch to get along with, instead of accepting that it is already within yourself. You are the master. You master those things. And that is possible in all walks of life and we are beginning to recognize that as we learn to rise out of our negative conditions or consciousness. Gradually, we are learning that it has been of no value to us, so why keep it up? The value is to *know* and *be* that very thing that you pronounce, and from there on you will continue to go ahead.

Nearly all of the people who are going ahead with these different plans take that attitude today. It is so with better than ninety per cent of the inventions coming out today. And see what we are accomplishing today. We are accomplishing more and have accomplished more in the last six years than we did in the eighty years previous.

Now I have been through those experiences and a little more than that and I know exactly how it has stepped up today, and it has stepped up for the very reason that we stand squarely on our feet and *know* that we *know* these things. They are there. If an invention was not already in existence, no one would ever get the frequency of the vibration that is set up to bring that into recognition. That frequency is there and the moment you train your mind and your thoughts, you will know exactly what you want to express. That is why we have gone ahead so remarkably today.

There are, of course, a great many avenues to that that hardly need any reference. So many people recognize that but those who do not recognize it should take particular pains to know that they *do know* and stand squarely by that declaration. It is the declaration that brings you through every time.

It has often been said that there is nothing new in the universe, and that is true. If that were not true there would be no representative vibration that could be picked up so that one could think of a given thing. All of those fields are in certain vibratory influences. Our whole life is vibration and, of course, we segregate that to a certain extent, but when we begin to realize that we are capable of tuning in with those vibrations and making them our own, then all these things become perfectly natural to us. Almost every inventor today realizes that he is not recording or bringing out anything but what has already at some time been recorded in vibratory frequency. The same is true in literature. Every book ever written has at some time been recorded in vibratory frequency. No spoken word ever goes out of existence. All are in the field known as the field of energy or vibratory influence.

Love is a word that comes very close to the word "God" in vibratory influence and we know of thousands of healings that have been accomplished with its use. Every known disease gives way to the power of love as we send it out. It builds such remarkable pictures or patterns around individuals, too. You can almost see where people give out love. It is like an armor about them.

A doctor friend of mine was appointed registrar of a Sioux Indian Reservation years ago. I was there on a visit and he invited me to come and see a test to be made by what we call the Medicine Man of the tribe; however, he proved to be no ordinary medicine man. This man went away by himself and remained in meditation for five years and when he came out of that meditation he was ready for the healing service.

He started slowly with the first test that was made. He put his arm into a kettle of boiling water and selected a piece of meat from that kettle. The hand came out unharmed. I knew this man for over two months after this test and there was no evidence whatever of any harm to his hand.

In the second test, he stood quietly, at a distance, before three of the best marksmen of the tribe. Dr. N— — and I took the bullets out of the cartridges, removed the powder and put in new powder, so that we knew there was no fake about it. Each one of those bullets flattened on that man's chest. I still have two of those flattened bullets in my possession.

After this man took his position in his little tepee, anyone with any deformity, disease or illness who came to him would leave completely healed. We saw that repeatedly. I became well acquainted with him and asked what his expression was and he replied that it was similar to the way we expressed divine love. That man is still living and he has gone on with his great healing work. We never read about him in the papers. He lives in absolute retirement and never comes out to talk about his work. He once said: "It is my place in life to give to people every attitude of love that I can express and thereby I receive my great reward." There is a Sioux Indian that very few people have ever heard of, performing a true service of Divine Love, silently, selflessly.

In Texas, a number of years ago, I heard stories of a little girl, five years old, who was a natural healer, through love. I went down to meet her and her mother told me the child was always telling everybody that she loved them. She would say, "I see that love all around everybody and around myself." Whenever she heard of anyone who was ill, she would ask her mother to take her to them and in almost every instance where she was taken into the room of the sick person, that one would get right up out of bed, perfectly well. That child has gone on to develop and she is doing a great work today.

There are many such instances. I knew a child in Holland. In Holland they have the red clover. It stands up about fifteen or sixteen inches above the ground, with beautiful blossoms. The clover is just about level with the porch floor of the farm house. I was visiting there one Sunday afternoon and we were sitting on the front porch, when that child walked right out across that field of clover for about thirty yards, right on those heads of clover. She never touched the ground with her feet, she just walked out, turned around and came back and stepped onto the porch.

We asked the child how she accomplished that. She said, "I don't know, I just give love to everything. I love that clover and that clover holds me up." And we found that she did. She talked about her playmates and said that she *loved* them all and they loved her, and so nothing could happen to them. I knew this girl until she was twenty-one years old. She moved into Belgium at that time and there I lost track of her. Her father told me that the only word he had ever heard her use was love for everybody.

And that *love* heals! Each one of us can do the same thing. It is so simple to radiate that great love out to everyone, even as those children did.

When I was in Spain, at one of the largest copper mines in the world, a Russian family with a little girl eleven years old moved over there and the father was working in the mine. They told me their child had what was known as the "healing touch." She would put her hand on a person and say, "I love you and I love you so much that your illness has passed away; it is gone. I have filled that space with love," and we found that to be true. In the case of a deformity, the body would become absolutely perfect. I saw a person in almost the last stages of epilepsy. This girl put her hand on that individual and said, "Your whole body is full of love and I see only the Light." In less than three minutes that malady was gone completely. The light and love emanating from her being were so powerful we could actually see it and feel it.

When I was a small boy I was playing with some of the children just outside our home in Cocanada, India. Darkness was approaching very rapidly, for in that country there is no twilight. One little boy picked up a stick and hit me across the arm and broke both bones and my hand fell right back. Of course, at first it was terribly painful and then my thoughts went to a statement I had been given by my teacher, "Go into the darkness and put your hand in the hand of God, for that is better than a light and safer than a known way." The Light just surrounded me and almost instantly that pain vanished completely. I climbed up into a great banyan tree, to be alone, and the light still surrounded me. I looked at it as a Presence but I'll never forget the incident and, as I sat there alone in that tree, that hand righted itself. I remained up in that tree all night. The next morning there was no sign of a break except for a ridge around the two bones which had been broken. Now my parents thought I had been cared for and put to bed by the servants. When I told them next morning what had happened they couldn't believe it and took me to a doctor immediately. He said the bones had been broken, but were knitted perfectly now. From that day on the hand never bothered me.

I merely cite a few of these instances as examples because they are so simple and so natural that all may do the same. I have seen where the building itself responded to the love poured out by an entire audience.

As the immortal Gautama Buddha has said: "To give five minutes to the realization of true divine love is greater than to pass a thousand bowls of food to the needy because, in giving forth love, you help every soul in the universe."

It melts right down, of course, to the words we use

91

and the thoughts and feelings we have. Words are things. Thoughts are things. Where your thoughts are, you are. When we learn to discipline and control our thoughts and feelings, and use only the positive, constructive words, sent forth with divine love, our body and mind respond to that righteousness — right-use-ness. The right use and selection of words is of vital importance but equally important is the feeling behind those words, for feeling is the motivating power that makes the words live. This is where divine love enters in. It doesn't mean we are to go around saying, "love, love, love." We speak the words once, with feeling, with vision, with conviction, with acceptance, and instantly the law moves into action to bring it into fulfillment. "Before ye have spoken I have answered." It is already there. In the words of Buddha: "Use love, concentrate upon it, treat yourself with love morning, noon, and night. As you sit down to partake of your food, use love, think it, feel it, and your food will taste a lot better."

There are many gems given forth by Buddha which have never been printed. The Poet, Tagore, used many of them in his writings. He was a man who knew how to use and express Love. He *knew* it. He *was*. He *is*.

"Love is far the most important thing of all. It is the golden gate of Paradise. Pray for the understanding of love; meditate upon it daily. It casts out fear; it is the fulfillment of the law; it conquers multitudes of sins. Love is abundantly invisible. Love

92

will conquer all. There is no disease that enough love will not heal today. No door that enough love will not open. No gulf that enough love will not bridge. No wall that enough love will not throw down. No sin that enough love will not redeem." — (from the Cloud of the Unknowing)

QUESTIONS AND ANSWERS

Q. I know a doctor who spent seven or eight years in India. When he returned to this country he challenged the County Medical Society. He asked them to present their test tubes containing the most virulent typhoid and other germs. He drank an amount sufficient to kill a young army and nothing came of it. I found out afterward that it was the conscious control of the thyroid. He apparently controlled the machinery of immunity.

A. Yes, it can be carried to immunity to every disease.

Q. How does the voluntary control of the thyroid gland affect acidity, so essential in warding off the effects of bacteria?

A. Acidity is controlled, to a great extent, with the voluntary control of the thyroid gland. It can be directed and stimulated to the extent that it controls acidity to an almost unlimited degree. I have heard a number of Hindus say that that is the reason they can control the bacteria. Acidity simply kills them off. The thyroid is stimulated with certain exercises that must be given by one versed in this teaching. Their mode is to stimulate the thyroid until it presents the proper amount of the fluid for the body's use.

Q. Do the parathyroids have any use?

A. Yes. The parathyroids are a very great adjunct. They control the metabolism of calcium or lime. They can be stimulated until calcium can be brought into the system to create a new set of teeth at any time.

Q. How are they stimulated?

A. The important element of their stimulation is concentration on the thyroid through a spiritual influence and that is exactly what we are talking about.

Q. Can you bring that into the realm of oxidation and the control of breathing?

A. With the breathing should be the spiritual exercises as well. That is, the exercise of the thought through the spiritual application.

Q. By concentration, do you mean the visualization of the thyroid working perfectly?

A. Yes, in perfect order and perfect harmony.

Q. Is there not something of a definite association between respiration and the thyroid action, also oxidation, through posture and breathing exercises?

A. Yes, that is the reason why posture and breathing exercises are given, to bring the whole activity of the body under spiritual influence. However, no teacher will give these exercises without

95

the spiritual activity, bringing the spiritual thought into activity as well. Many people can bring those spiritual activities into function and active use almost instantly because of some special influence which has been brought to bear.

Q. What of the adrenals?

A. The adrenals have to do with the blood pressure. The thyroid gland controls all of the others. The thyroid is controlled by the pituitary and that by the pineal. That is why you must become as a little child. In post mortem examinations the pineal is found to be atrophied to a large extent. In such cases we are divorced from the Kingdom of Heaven. The pineal is the prime center for controlling all of the endocrines. It is the Master, the I AM of the physical body.

A. Do not some of the great Masters discuss this subject of improved action of the endocrines from the standpoint of prana and breathing?

A. Their attitude is that if you are accepting prana you are accepting the spiritual influences. They come right back to the spiritual influences. That is the greatest activity and activator. They claim that is what activates the thought of youth. Then the pituitary and pineal will come into action immediately.

Q. Would you not infer that Jesus had definitely taught His disciples this system of working on the endocrines?

A. Yes, through the Christian method, which is Love in action. He could say readily that if you would become as a little child you would enter the Kingdom of Heaven.

Q. Are these material scientists who are discovering the modern miracles of bio-chemistry inspired by the Masters?

A. Yes, the work is being given out through these people to the race for the benefit of mankind.

CHAPTER VII

THE REALITY

THE HINDU says: "If God wished to hide, God would choose man to hide in." That is the last place man would look for God.

The trouble with the masses of humanity today is that they are trying to become something that is already right within. We are seeking and searching everywhere outside ourselves for God, attending countless lectures, meetings, groups; reading innumerable books; looking to teachers and personalities and leaders, when all the time God is right within. If mankind will let go of the *trying* and accept that they *are,* they will soon be perfectly aware of the Reality.

Jesus told us so many times that there is no one any different from another, that each is a God-being, with all the potential attributes and qualifications.

We have set Jesus aside for so long, thinking that He was in a different category than ourselves. He is no different. He never claimed to be. He goes about assisting mankind all of the time. He is no mythical character any more than we are mythical characters and in no way did He ever claim to be able to perform a miracle. They were not miracles, they were merely the fulfillment of natural law. That has been proved today. They were natural occurrences that must and will transpire for anyone if we fulfill the law.

Each one of us is capable of mastering every one of the so-called difficulties we are working under and, the moment we let go of them, they cease to exist. That may seem incredible to many but it is an absolute fact. We bring these things upon ourselves by our own transverse thoughts.

Supposing those thoughts, those words, never belonged to us, that we had never heard of them, that they had no existence in our vocabulary or our world. We know of four different languages today where there is not a negative word in the language, there is not a word in the past tense, or a word in the future tense. All is here and now, accomplished. If we could realize and accept that, we would soon rise out of our negative conditions. It is the name that we give a thing and the feeling with which we release it. Negative words, feelings, conditions have absolutely no power except what we individually give to them. The moment we cease feeding our energy into them, they no longer have life, and thus they cease to exist.

We have proved conclusively today that because of the word "God" registered in the Bible, that book has maintained as it has. It has the greatest sale of any book in the world today. Now if that word will maintain a book, an inanimate thing, what will it do through our use of it through our own body form? It is not necessary to go around repeating the word "God, God." Just send that word forth once with definite, sincere meaning and qualified with what that expression is intended to bring about and you will never have to repeat it. Why? Because you are right in that very sound track of vibration that sets up every response to your statement. That is the reason the Bible is maintained and we carry on with just that one word with its emphasis. Then the important one word with its emphasis. Then the important thing is not to negate it but hold positively to the fulfillment of our statement.

Now certain individuals in India will go around with their hands up in the air saying, "Om mani padme Om." In a little while the hand grows there and they can't bring it down. It would be just the same if we ran around here saying, "God, God," all the time. We can think the word and know definitely that it is ours; we are that very thing we wish to express and we don't need to repeat it over and over at all. We simply *are* that.

It has been said that man's greatest mistake is in trying to *become* God instead of simply *being*. He has been looking for something that is right within himself. We don't *try* to become, we must simply *be* it; we *are* it, and we *claim* it definitely. If you don't really believe that, you try it some time, for say two weeks. I would suggest you say it once, and *know* it, and then go on and *be* it. It is yours. It is yours to command.

Heaven is the everywhere present harmony within the individual, right where you are. You have the free will, through your own thought and feeling, to make it hades if you want to and you don't have much trouble doing it but, if you will spend the time you expend in attempting to bring hades in creating and bringing heaven right here and now, you will have the manifestation of it.

Know God within, always. There is the greatest blessing for humanity. See the other fellow the same as you see yourself — the Christ in every face. This is our greatest privilege. Not only that, it is the greatest training for us just to see the Christ in every person we see or know. It takes only a moment to realize that in every company you are in and you will find it is a marvelous thing. Soon you will come to realize and accept the Christ within each and every one. We are all the same, in His likeness, always.

Referring again to negative words, thoughts, and feelings, we know of 2500 people today who are associated together, who have traveled on every known means of conveyance and over thousands and thousands of miles and they have never had an accident. Most of these people are right here in America where the association had its inception. It was started by four people.

You are in control of the storms; you are in control of the atmospheric conditions, every one of you. You are in control of every natural element. It doesn't matter what it is, you are the master of it, and it is for you to become master of it. Instead of that, we let it get us down, as we say, and we become subordinate to the condition, or situation, or circumstance. There is not one person in this room who, if he would step forth, could not master every situation that arises, simply by *knowing* that he is the master.

Animals are very sensitive to these things. They respond when you give them thoughts of kindness.

They even recognize when you send out thoughts of kindness to others. The dog recognizes feelings immediately.

We had over 1100 dogs in Alaska for our mail routes there. We had the mail routes up there for a long time. We used over 1100 dogs, before the planes came in and, do you know, every one of our men came to the point where they never used a whip. Those dogs were just as tractable as could be, just as long as the men did not disturb or upset them.

I made nine trips with dogs over that trail, a distance of 1800 miles. Twice I never changed a dog and still those dogs came through in very wonderful shape. Everybody asked how I did it. I just let the dogs alone, urged them on, told them that they were all right, going ahead doing fine, and so on. The other men began doing that and it made a great difference. If you do not fear an animal or mistreat it but praise it and encourage it, it will respond wonderfully.

The moment we use a negative word we are taking energy from our body to keep it going; we hypnotize ourselves into believing that is a fact and that hypnotic influence is what carries us right on to repeat it again and again. Now, if we no longer permit ourselves to become hypnotized by those negative thoughts and refuse ever to repeat them again or even to think them, they disappear from our worlds completely.

If we would let go of old age, lack of eyesight, and imperfections in the body, these negative conditions would not register in the physical form. Our body is being renewed all the time and that is really the resurrection. That resurrection takes place every nine months throughout all of humanity. We put the imprint upon those body cells ourselves by our own thoughts, our own feelings, our own speech. We are our own betrayers. We betray the Christ with the simple word "can't" every time we use the word. Every time we use a negative word we betray the Christ within ourselves. Let us, therefore, extol the Christ, bless the body for its service, give praise and thanks for our countless blessings, and *be* the living manifestation of the Law every moment!

QUESTIONS AND ANSWERS

Q. How do the Hindus look upon Jesus as compared with Buddha?

A. They say that Buddha was the Way to Enlightenment but that the Christ *is* Enlightenment.

Q. Why does it seem so difficult to hold the mind to an ideal?

A. We have not the definite training which those in the East have had. There, even the children have it. They are shown that when one ideal is projected they are to keep that ideal until they have its full accomplishment. The training in the Western world is somewhat different. We are allowed to let every thought come running through, scattering our forces. If you have an ideal and fully believe in it, keep it entirely to yourself, not mentioning it to another until it is completely consolidated into form. Always keep the mind clear for that one thing which you MUST accomplish — not that which you WILL. That keeps the mind clear. The moment we allow another thought to come in we become "dual minded." By expressing energy toward that one ideal we become single minded. Nor would we get into a rut or become "one track" minded, for we would not need to dwell on that ideal for more than an instant if we directed every force toward it and did not scatter our forces. From then on we simply give thanks that it is accomplished and that it is here and now.

Q. Are we to understand that you personally saw and even shook hands with Jesus?

A. Yes. And with many so-called Masters. Those people do not claim to be different from you or me. Even the coolies in India recognize Him as Jesus of Nazareth. There is nothing mysterious about it. The pictures show Him as an ordinary man with a great light about Him. There is nothing vague about any of these people. There is a very definite determination about them — they are vivid characters.

Q. How is it that the ordinary coolie in India sees Jesus?

A. The coolie has accepted it and lives with it, whereas we live in a condition in which we do not accept or believe that He exists. Now I have no psychic sight whatever. If we deal wholly in principle, we cannot be misguided. Intuition is a factor and we must make it *knowing*.

Q. Why has Jesus not appeared often in America?

A. He does not localize Himself and undoubtedly works here as much as in India.

Q. Did Jesus suffer physically on the cross?

A. No. One so highly illumined could not suffer

physically. If he had not wished to go through that experience he could have sent back the energy and it would have destroyed the people about to crucify him. He showed the way.

Q. Did Jesus exist for a number of years on this earth after the crucifixion?

A. We know of no withdrawal from the body on his part. He lives today in that very body. That body is observable by anyone who comes in contact with it.

Q. Do you mean that an individual known as Jesus of Nazareth has appeared in this country?

A. Yes. Naturally, if we do not call Him by that name, He will not be here to us.

Q. Is it through some special consideration that you are able to give out the teaching of the Masters?

A. We are not privileged in any way over you yourself. When asked if there are Masters in the United States, They reply that there are over one hundred and fifty million masters here.

Q. Would Jesus appear here if we needed Him?

A. He is always where He is needed. When He said, "Lo, I Am with you always," He meant just that.

Q. Does Christ mean the principle of life?

A. It means God-principle flowing through the individual.

CHAPTER VIII

MASTERY OVER DEATH

"**D**EAD YOGI still lives!" read the headlines in Los Angeles papers, in reporting the passing of Paramhansa Yogananda, founder of the Self Realization Fellowship in Los Angeles, California.

"Mortuary technicians today revealed the amazing story of Paramhansa Yogananda as his body lay in state at Self Realization headquarters here. They say his body is still not technically dead twenty days after his death. The mortuary director of the cemetery declared that the body of Yogananda, who died during a speech at the Biltmore Hotel, was under daily observation by his staff from March 7 to March 27, when the bronze casket was sealed. 'The absence of any visual signs of decay in the dead body of Paramhansa Yogananda offers the most extraordinary case in our experience,' said the mortuary director in a notarized letter to Self Realization Fellowship."

Now in reference to Yogananda's body, that was not a miracle. We have seen bodies that have been lying in suspended animation, it has been claimed, for six hundred years. My great, great grandfather observed such a body a long time ago. That is just north of the line between Kashmir and the Pakistan of today, and it has been there ever since. That body, of course, was laid down as a sign of the

109

displeasure aroused in India, first by the Mohamme-
dan invasion, then child marriage, and also the deep
caste system that invaded India. It has lain there
ever since. It is about fourteen years since I last saw
the body; also, I was in the vicinity during the first
World War. At that time there were about 200
British soldiers trapped in the mountains north of
this place and they asked for safe transportation
through this country, and as they came out into
India again they observed this body. The Captain
had spent a great many years in India and had a
great respect for the Hindu people, and they also
respected him. He explained to his soldiers that, if
they wished to observe this body, the company would
halt here to see it, but they must give their word of
honor that they would not attempt to touch the
body, thus conforming to the wish of the people in
that community. So many people have gone to view
that body that the flagstones that lie around the
canopy where this body is lying are worn through.

After the soldiers had seen the body, they moved
on a short distance and made their camp for the
night. After the camp was ready, one of the Ser-
geants asked the Captain for leave. (I had this directly from the Captain.) He said to the Sergeant: "I
believe I know what you wish to do. You are going to
attempt to touch that body. Now, unless you give me
your word of honor that you will not attempt to
touch it, I will refuse you the leave." The Sergeant
gave his word, he got his leave, and went up to
observe the body. At that time the officers carried
what is known as a little quirt. He walked up to the

body and attempted to touch it with that quirt and he fell dead! The Captain told me I was the first one to be notified and, of course, my first thought was that someone was watching and had shot the man in revenge, but the Captain said he went there immediately and made a thorough examination of the soldier's body and there wasn't a mark on it. This experience was reported to the War Department in London and is on file there today.

In our laboratory we have made experiments with the condition called death. The tests have not been our own developments but have been carried out by a camera taking thousands of exposures a second. An image is imposed upon a running point of light. When photographed, the film records an assembly of points of light from which we get the completed image. This is then reproduced under high magnification and slowed down until it can be thrown on an ordinary screen. It can then be x-rayed, showing the complete formation of a life element.

Many have come to us with a malady where they knew they had only a few more hours to live, volunteering themselves for observation. A physician in charge observes the time when what is ordinarily described as death takes place. A scale records a loss in weight of about eleven ounces. The light emanation from the body is shown just above the scale.

Today we know the life element has intelligence, movement, and volition to the extent that if we put an interference over it, it will go right up through the interference. It will go on up through the ceiling. We have checked this by variously placing four cameras. When a camera on the floor lost it, an upper one picked it up and showed that there was still evidence of the emanation of energy. We put the interference over it again and moved it to the side. The emanations went through the wall. When the camera on one side lost the emanation, the camera on the other side picked it up.

We built a cone-shaped interference of aluminum, lead foil and asbestos to fit down over the body in an attempt to prevent the life element from escaping. In three instances, in less than one minute after we had closed the interference, the body came to life. When that life returned, the body had no semblance of the disease which it had before and it was evidently immune to that disease. We do not know why.

We have a group experimenting with it now, and we look into the future when it will be shown that the reason why the life element has taken on greater energy is so that, when it returns to a body, new conditions will be established. The three of whom I spoke all had the black plague. One of them now goes out to work with the black plague to show that he is immune. One is afraid of it and we have not urged him to go out, yet it is seven years since the change and he has never contracted it again. The third man has no understanding at all of what we are doing so that he is of no help.

Before this life element leaves the body we can show that the vibrations are so lowered that the life element cannot remain, it is crowded out completely. But, when it is crowded out, it has this volition that has been created with it and it begins to assimilate energy. Thus in a very short time it can assume a new body under any conditions. We cannot say positively that this is a fact but we believe that many bodies are reassembled in from one to three hours after the experiment of death.

In the case of the body lying in suspended animation for six hundred years, it was suggested that this man was actively functioning in another body. We finally came to the place where this man was living with his supposed second body. We took his photograph and compared it with one of the body in suspended animation and there was an exact resemblance.

Again, we saw another of his bodies. In all, we found four different bodies. We know that many transport their bodies from place to place far more quickly than we could travel. So we arranged for four cameras in the hands of four men who could not be influenced and set them so that they could take photographs at exactly the same time. When we brought these photographs together, there was an identical resemblance between all four and the body lying in suspended animation. They were the same pattern.

We have been told thousands of times that bodies are reassembled and, if a person lives a definite life, when that condition of death comes about, he can lay one body down and assemble a new one instantly.

Thus we see why we should think differently of

passing through death. It is a condition that we have brought upon ourselves so that we may pass into a greater condition with greater possibilities.

Jesus often told us that we become that which we worship. If we find ourselves in limitation, we have worshipped limitation. Yet there isn't a human being who cannot worship perfection and by that attitude bring himself out of limitation.

It is said today that the human body can resist any condition. If we stand with thought directing the God principle, we bring into play the power that surrounds us and so consolidate it that nothing can touch us.

Perfection is always in existence, is always active and, when we stand one with it, it operates instantly. In many instances we see the very light emanating from the person's body, and when photographs are taken the light can be seen in the pictures. Light is life or that medium in which life exists.

It is quite evident that if, instead of placing old age as the goal, as we do, we placed youth there and stepped forward in a determined, positive attitude, we would accomplish that state. Men and women today are achieving eternal youth. Many Eastern philosophers say, "If you would worship youth, beauty, purity, and perfection as definitely as you worshipped old age, you would accomplish that condition. In fact, you could not do otherwise." This is not, by any means, to decry old age, but it is to show the attitude of thought that brings it on. Would it not be better to reverence men for the youth, beauty, and measure of perfection they express rather than for old age? The very ideal belongs to a body widely accepted as created in the image of its Maker. The divinity that man accepts as belonging to him reaches its highest expression in youth, beauty, and purity.

We project conditions for ourselves to follow. We all admit that we can use it with the wrong attitude. But if we work toward perfection, perfection must result. No one accomplishes anything unless he becomes one with the object, forgetting all other conditions. Bringing it down to a very simple fact, if we state definite, positive ideas for ourselves to accomplish, then we do accomplish those very conditions readily. One point! One direction! Never allow the thought to vary for an instant to any negative condition.

We have seen many changes and healings, positive conditions brought out of negative surroundings, without a word being spoken. This has been evidence to us that the principle does manifest with every attitude of positive thought. But the thoughts must always be conclusively positive. Those who have developed the power to accomplish these things at will we know as Masters because they have mastered the forces of nature. They do not deal with conditions as if perfection were a rare phenomenon. Perfection is a natural state which may be attained by following natural conclusions — always!

This body is indestructible. We ourselves allow this body to be destroyed. The very thoughts and feelings we impose upon the body are the creators of age, disease, and disintegration. It is well known today that every cell in our bodies is renewed in less than a year. One of the greatest fallacies ever imposed upon humanity is the three score years and ten! We know men and women who are over 2,000 years old. Now if one can live 2,000 years, he can live for eternity. That is exactly what Jesus meant when He said "The last enemy to be overcome is death."

Jesus taught that the Father is the principle by which humanity might accomplish, that Life must live, that there is no mystery in His deeds and teachings.

Principle cannot change. You can overlook it for eternity if you will, but the moment you return to it you will return to perfect condition. Your body takes on the result of that determination. One knowing and using that principle would not hesitate to walk upon the water. You have often been told that if one endeavors to accomplish and succeeds, all can. The power has always existed and always will exist. Why is it kept away? Because we put up the barrier of disbelief.

The power that brings into existence a mechanical device could instantly bring into being the condition that device produces. We talk across great distances with the telephone. There are many people, however, who talk over great distances without any device whatever. Telepathy is recognized as an established fact. There is a great power contained in mental telepathy. It is God speaking to God. There are many who may say such a statement is sacrilegious. Such a statement is just as definite as the statement that we are living today. Humanity must ultimately learn that it is far better to live in positive influences at all times. Then we will take the great step forward.

These are not conclusions of our group alone. Many people and groups are working along the same lines. Use of these facts will bring us into complete harmony, complete unity, where man has accomplished.

Now it does not make any difference whether the body of humanity believes these things today. The facts are evident. When Jesus said He had overcome death, He spoke truly. Thousands upon thousands today, seeing the truth, will know that this body is immortal, pure, perfect, and indestructible. The mystery is gone and we are on the threshold of complete understanding.

QUESTIONS AND ANSWERS

Q. Do you know of anyone other than the Masters who has attained complete mastery over old age and death?

A. Yes, many people have accomplished this. You yourself may do it. *Know* you are the master of it and you are. I have seen people come right back, I know probably sixty, who were grey haired and old in appearance. They let go of all thought of birthdays, all thought of age, and today they look about forty.

Q. What can we do with children when they go to school where they are taught one way, the church another way, and we teach Truth at home? Will they not be confused?

A. You can help your children so they will not be confused with the Truth. You can give very simple statements of Truth to the children and they will take them and they will go deeper than any other statements, i.e., "The Christ is right within you." You will see what the children will answer finally about it. Children, many of them, have a greater measure of perception than adults realize.

Q. In Volume III you state in effect that we can raise our vision just a little higher and literally see Jesus, if our attention is turned within.

118

A. When you see the Christ, you will know that it is the same as Jesus, and that Christ is in everyone, every place, when you become associated.

Q. Have you actually seen and conversed with Jesus or was it a mental apparition?

A. No, it was not an apparition. The man is living and real and we can photograph Him just as we can photograph you.

Q. Man being essentially a spiritual being and constantly seeking the light, how will he be able to recognize Truth in our modern age when there are so many different beliefs and teachings and so much opposition?

A. Man is spirit. It doesn't matter what opposition we put up to spirit. Man *is*, always. There is no opposition to that; only our thoughts are in opposition.

Q. Is it true when we call on the Christ for help that He is with us and that He hears?

A. These are His words regarding this: "Call upon the Christ within." That is nearer to you—that *is* you. Call upon the Christ within. He doesn't mind our calling upon Him because He is working all the time with humanity. We make the error of looking without for the Christ. First call upon the Christ within, always. Then it extends right out to the whole universe and whatever we call for is ours.

CHAPTER IX

THE LAW OF SUPPLY

THE repetition of mantrams is hypnotic and people set their own limitations by leaning on the power of affirmation.

The moment we say, "I want a certain condition," we have barred the way to much good that we did not recognize and have opened but one avenue of expression. Unless the statement were in accord with the fullness of an expanding life, the realization might take a form not anticipated. The very emphasis on want may aggravate the need instead of granting supply. The moment we put up a bar to the free flow of substance by a limiting statement, we hinder the perfect expression of God's abundance.

What is the great expression that brings all things? "I AM abundance." This statement opens every avenue of expression and closes none. It recognizes the presence of God in all things and the conscious unity of the self with the source of all good. You will find that this was the teaching of Jesus. It was abundance always, with no limitation whatever.

"I AM knowledge." "I AM harmony." Use of these expressions will vitalize the energy in the body so that there results a new awareness of the abundance of knowledge and harmony. Nor is the energy depleted through free use in daily life.

But if one has abundance, others must have it. As we assume that attitude we shall come to know that if one does not have abundance, none can be prosperous. If we believe we are not prosperous, it is because we have isolated ourselves from this freely flowing abundance and built up the idol of lack.

We have made believe we are just a part of the whole. But everyone is merged in the whole because there is completion only in that unity. If one were out, it could not be complete. The moment we realize our unity with the completed condition, we find that we express it outwardly.

Worship of God with all our hearts and all our strength frees us from conditions of limitation. No one need be isolated. It is possible to realize that sense of union with God's abundance right now. The first determination must be an effort to get rid of the individual sense of limitation that we ourselves have built. There are several rather definite steps that must be taken to free the self from limitation.

There is no situation that cannot be conquered. Happiness, prosperity, and abundance belong to all. The greatest bar is the lack of acceptance.

When the rabble scoffed at Jesus did He pay any attention? When He saw people searching for things they thought belonged to them He told them to stand still and see the salvation of the Lord. He went on to explain that man is the lord of all creation. He said, "Peace be still," and He taught His disciples to "recognize that you are free." With that declaration they brought themselves from what was considered the lowly walks of life into their discipleship. When

Jesus chose a disciple from among fishermen, did He see him as a fisherman? No. He saw him as His disciple, a "fisher of men." He said, "Follow me." He instructed them to follow the expressions that had brought Him to where He was. All was done with the greatest humility because He made it plain that self-ishness could not enter into the Kingdom of Heaven.

Perspective on the conditions throughout the earth today shows that seeming discord puts us in a position where we think that we are separate from our neighbor and only unrelated individuals in the great plan of existence. But no one body can be taken out of that plan and the plan continue to manifest. Every individual is just as necessary to its completion as the number of atoms to the molecule. When, through our expressions we again show the unison of existence, we realize that we were never separate nor outside of a unity with the whole.

Jesus taught in simple terms that the object of this life is not death but a greater expression of life. Every one is a unit in the whole principle operating in harmony, where every individual stands in his own domain, completely in accord. For that reason you will find if you go through the simple teachings of Jesus that He put forth the declaration, "I AM God," for every individual to use. That is not a part of the Principle but the Principle itself.

Religious doctrines have all too often emphasized theory instead of practice. Repetition of such an attitude limits our understanding of Truth to the physical things and we lose the spiritual significance. When Jesus was asked regarding the answering of prayer, He said that the reason prayer was not answered was that the asking had been amiss. You will find that if you stand definitely with a positive declaration, you will not need to use words at all. The moment that you realize within yourself that abundance already exists for you, at that very instant the condition manifests for you. Then you do not need outside suggestion. You are in perfect harmony with Principle. The instant you think of any condition you are one with it. You will find that if you stand definitely with a situation, you will never need to repeat a petition. It is finished before you ask. Jesus said, "While they are asking I have heard." Then He went right on and said, "Before it is spoken it is already accomplished."

Do we need to go on asking for a condition that is already accomplished? How many times can a condition be completed? Need we beg for something that is already ours? No! You can trace the lives of our greatest men and see how they accepted accomplishment. Deep in the subconscious the way of accomplishment already existed. With freedom from any sense of limitation they were able to express that which already existed.

It is through complete lack of division that we stand as Principle. How could we be in want if we put God in the place of want? Principle is harmonious and flows according to definite laws with which man must learn to work.

QUESTIONS AND ANSWERS

Q. You say that we should never go back to the asking for anything we may want.

A. That always implies doubt. If we go right on we are above every doubt and fear. If it was not already accomplished we would never think of it.

Q. In other words, seek and know and draw a mental picture of the completion?

A. Yes, absolutely. If we look to Divine Mind for the solution we open every avenue. If we project ourselves, we close every avenue except ourselves. The self makes mistakes. The other never does.

Q. Why can't we hold out our hands as the Masters do and have them filled?

A. Because we will not do it. It is just because we say we cannot see it. Put out your hands and give thanks. That is what Elijah did. It is being done today in millions of forms.

Q. In what way have the Masters helped you in your work?

A. I can say that had it not been for Their assistance the work could not even have been started, let alone be carried on. We have never had to go to any organization or individual outside of our own family group. Had it not been for Their assistance we would not have been able to carry on, even had we had the finances. We have gone on many times according to our own deductions but, in every instance, we have had to come back to Their conclusions, which are based upon the knowledge of chemistry and mechanical devices preserved from ancient civilizations.

CHAPTER X

"THE TRUTH SHALL MAKE YOU FREE"

JESUS told us that the Truth would make us free. When one stands in that free, flowing stream of universal power, nothing can touch him, let alone hinder or stop him.

The Christ is God flowing through the individual. One standing in that attitude has everything to use and all of the Principle flows through him.

Why has this power become static, inactive, and non-responsive in so many of us? Only because of our own attitude toward it. Each individual's attitude of thought can completely check the utilization of it, even though it continues to flow in universal abundance. When one is aware of this power flowing through him, he can give conscious expression to it.

When Jesus made the statement regarding His unity with the Father, He knew that all humanity could be as He was and is. The Truth frees us from any negative condition in which we may be involved. We alone bring about those negative conditions and we alone can free ourselves from them by changing our thoughts. Jesus knew the science of expressing that freedom. He knew that humanity would go on to greater and greater accomplishment as more individuals grasped the Truth.

We are just beginning to realize our possibilities. All through the scientific world changes are coming about. Scientists are learning that if they will definitely work with Principle they will accomplish their research more effectively and quickly. That attitude is taking their work out of the guessing state.

The debasement of God is death. There is no death except through the debasement of God. Jesus showed us the way to turn to God. "Worship God with all your heart, with all your soul, with all your mind, and with all your strength." In debasement we have worshipped outside conditions and made every idol possible and worshipped them. Man must bring forth God from within, in that way presenting God to the whole world.

Many people have asked where we get our authority for our statements. You can find it for yourself by taking a Jewish Bible and a lexicon and making your own translation. You will find a complete story of millions of years of evolution in the first chapter of Genesis. We find that there have been great epochs of humanity. Through the distortion of the original teachings, humanity has been taught that it was outside of God's dispensation, living in a material condition through which it must work. But God never cast man outside of Himself. Man himself has built the illusion of a mortal existence wherein God must be won by prayer and acceptance of religious formalities.

Yet, no matter what attitude we take, we cannot alter Perfection. It stands pre-eminent. It does not matter to Principle into what form you build this body with your thoughts. You do not alter Principle in any way by building what you think of as an imperfect body. We can entertain all the doubts we wish but some day the truth will sink in. When we drop all our doubts we are back in Perfection where we belong. Jesus told us that we are our own saviors. How could a completed love forgive anything? How could completed Principle forgive anything? It is only that we forgive ourselves from this separation.

This great race of today is right at the point of accepting the great order of the Christ — the Christ in the individual. Can't we see that if we turn completely to the Christ Principle, presenting the Christ-like attributes instead of destructive thoughts, we should become so aware of this great condition that we would change the nature of all humanity! We are face to face with it now. When we accept, we shall know it as we are known.

This great period in which we are today is the completion of the cycle where the Christ stands forth again dominant. The Christ always stands as the conqueror. The entire Bible is a complete bringing forth of that condition, pointing right to this time, with the Christ coming forth; meaning that every one of us presents the Christ.

The moment we accept, this body becomes a light body. Then we begin to use the power of which we have been unaware for so long.

****

We have now passed through the so-called Golden Age of the natural philosopher, which reached its climax about 150 years ago. We are now fully aware of the wonders of nature and its projected perfect Divine Plan and that divinity is within every unit of all humanity. Also in every tree, every plant, every flower, as well as all vegetable life. While the minerals have life, they were formerly under an entirely different sphere of existing influence.

As all of humanity learn to use and bring into active control all of their mind faculties, they will find that there is within the mind every ability to control and fully create and bring into existence every atom and every planet. All substance then creates all substance into being. This factor is the supreme intelligence or God-Intelligence which moves upon and through all things and is the creator of all things. Man has stood in this Godhead for eternity, the actual ruler and creator of all things; but as one begins to deviate from this great and noble plan, then that thought may create a bug, a worm, or a vicious thing to move about and torment humanity and even destroy himself or a portion of humanity. But even if millions do use thoughts adversely, those thoughts will in no way affect the entire plan. They may apparently affect a seeming large portion of humanity, yet the full God balance holds all in complete accord and unfailingly to the original plan so that no atom is misplaced.

Then is it difficult to conceive how all come from the one cell as that point of Infinite Intelligence of humanity, that infinite divinity, rules all supreme over all and through all things? This Infinite Intelligence was ruling long before the universe began to appear as being. Then let us worship that great Intelligence as the one and only cause and ourselves as that very thing, as this will eventually bring us into a clear understanding of It as well as of all things.

Unless we cling tenaciously to this and accept it as absolute truth or fact, we will always miss the salient point of our complete existence. It is through the selectivity of the Divine emanating Principle that the Christ is born, it is the creation of the whole human race, the true Christ in every form. This is the immaculate, the true conception that Mary foresaw, and the total conception of every child born. The true Christ is perpetuated throughout all humanity. Thus all humanity is eternal and immortal, the true God being.

Look at the wonders of creation and birth. Go back 800 million years, if you wish, and you will find this God Principle, the Christ in each and every individual dominant among all humanity. Trace on down to the present and you will find it just as commanding, just as dominant, also just as justifiable as it was at that age. It matters not how it has been covered by man's ignorant, negative, or mortal thinking. The moment one glimpses this all-sustained and sustaining Truth, the entire thought current is open to its beneficient influence.

It is that very influence that has placed and sustained the heavy layer of oxygen just far enough above this earth that it is a protecting shield that filters out the life-giving rays from the sun and lets just enough come through to maintain life upon this planet. Just as soon as humanity sees this great beneficent action and what it means to each and every individual, then will the Christ principle again sweep through all humanity and they will see the one supreme God Intelligent Principle that governs justly, wisely, and completely. There will be no more of the setting up of false Gods or graven images.

This complete Truth or unity of purpose is never deviated from by storm or condition of emotion. It just stands steadfast above the storm. This great calm is in no wise affected for, again as we open our thought to its influence and just let it flow through our entire being, our thoughts are so saturated by its deifying influence that we soon find our mind is really at home again and we are one and the only instrument that has completely transcended time and space. We have arrived again in the beautiful garden of God Intelligent Principle; at home right here on earth where the beauties of all heaven really do and always have existed. The wonderful paradise of God within every human form.

Go directly within yourself to find God, the Supreme Intelligence. When you do this whole-heartedly and know that God is really you, the entire being of you, you will find every answer and you will be ever-permanent, stable, and all-knowing. There you will find that you are right at home; also you will find that you are all things, know all things, and capable of giving out all things and that you are all Truth. It is well to know that every individual is the same as you and to give them the same privileges that you have.

As you carry this to success and know that you have mastered all obstacles, you can go where you will, do as you will, and speak God forth into all things and there will be no limitations in your thoughts for others.

The only time it takes to make these transitions is the time that you allow; allow an instant and it is accomplished. Just rejoice in God, your very self, and free every limitation; also recall that one instant is all eternity.

"I thank you God for life and light abundant, full and free; for perfect abundance, wealth and power, and unhampered liberty."

In using this prayer, always think and keep your thoughts on your full and complete body temple and know that this body form that you see is God. When you are looking at your body you are looking at the complete and perfect God temple.

Your body is the very first temple that was ever brought forth into form. Therefore, it is the first and purest temple where God could dwell. Then why not love and worship this perfect God temple? For, by loving and worshipping it as a God-temple, perfect and complete, we must be absolutely aware of this body as the God temple complete, for *loving, thinking,* and *accepting* is true worship.

There never was a temple like this Temple of the living God. Every temple built by hands can in no way compare with this body temple. They are pictures and forms that the mind has thought out, conceived and built or brought into form. Yet they fall far short of even bringing forth one function of this beautiful body temple. There is not a laboratory in all the world that is capable of doing what this body laboratory does without taking any thought of the process: taking in food and transmuting it into life or bringing forth a living form that is perpetuating a race; or even flexing a muscle, let alone thinking, acting, moving, talking, and perceiving that which is the present, the past, or the future; the ability to construct, build, also to go forth and teach and endow accomplishments; to assist posterity; to give forth that which is good and noble, honorable, and magnificent.

Then think. Is there a temple aside from this body temple that can give forth all of these virtues, unless they are endowed with them by this great glorious body temple, the first and only temple not made by human hands? Is it any wonder that God chose to abide and be at home within this glorious body form; this form Divine; this God Temple body that completely renews itself!

Then let us cast about and see how and why this body has been so degraded. We have been taught by sacrilegious, deceitful, ignorant, profit-seeking individuals with but a smattering of the real truth, that this body is weak, sinful, imperfect, inferior, abnormal, subject to disease, decay and death; that it is conceived in iniquity and born in sin and every other thought and expression that immoral man can conjure up.

First let us think and look into the past and see and understand just where and how these teachings, thoughts, and words have gradually drawn us into the terrible vortex and miasma of sin, duplicity, sickness, failure, and last, the greatest dishonor of all, death. Let us view with a clear vision the results of this dishonest perfidy and see to what extent it has led us into the dishonor of this perfect God body form.

Then from that moment on let us truly forgive, thus, forget, and let it pass from our lives, our thoughts, our actions, and our whole experience. Again, let us keep forgiving and forgetting it until every vestige of the experience is completely erased from our subconscious thoughts. It is within the subconscious thought process that it has, by repetition, been engraved as in a photograph, through vibratory influence, until it repeats to us these records over and over, again and again, until we believe they are true.

The photograph of yourself or any friend or individual is but the record of the vibration of that body form. It is in this way that the thought forms or the forms of the spoken word in vibration are recorded in the subconscious and it has the ability to repeat it to you. Then let us think just for a moment how we have trained ourselves to accept and believe and worship these degrading untruths.

Then let us think or suppose, just for a moment, that we had never heard or been taught these words of untruth and that they had never been lodged into our vocabulary. We would never have known them or accepted or learned or believed or worshipped them.

If we are capable of learning them and believing them, we are far more capable of unlearning them by demanding that they leave every time they come up or are repeated to us from the subconscious. Just say to them, *"You are completely forgiven, so leave me entirely alone."* Then say to your subconscious, *"Just erase all of those and accept no record, only the truth as I set it forth."*

How can you express youth, beauty, purity, divinity, perfection, and abundance until you see, feel, hear, and know them and put them forth in thought, word, action, and expression, yes, by worshipping them. By so doing you impress them on or into your subconscious thought and this subconscious thought reflects these thoughts back to you from the pictures you have presented to it, through the vibration that you have established or set up there. You will soon find that it is no more trouble for the subconscious thought to repeat the truth that you are sending forth to it than it is to repeat the former untruths that you have previously imposed upon it. The more you impress the truth upon the subconscious by love and worship, the more it will send it back to you. This is where you are the master. For, by forgiving the untruths and letting go of them, you will find that you have mastered them. You are above and beyond them; they are forgiven and forgotten.

You will find by talking to your body, the subconscious of you, and *knowing* that what you are saying is the absolute truth, it outpictures. For, if this that you are telling your body is not the truth, you would not have a body, you would in no way be able to think, act, move, speak, feel, see, hear, breathe, or live.

Then the greatest privilege in the world is to know

that all are the same and have the same power that you have. That they, as well as you, have the same powers and that they, as well as you, have never lost that power. They, as well as you, may have perverted their thoughts about that power but those perverted thoughts have never in any way changed or diminished that power. For, when we change to true thoughts, words, and actions, we find that power flows through our body and we readily feel the glory of its response.

Yours is the power to do this completely. You have given limitation dominion over your thoughts. Simply break that shell that you have allowed yourself to be encased in and you are Freedom itself.

"Know the Truth, and the Truth shall make you free."

QUESTIONS AND ANSWERS

Q. Is it true that you were in India in person and experienced those things in the body as recorded in the books which you wrote?

A. We have never, in any way, been able to travel in the astral condition and have used no method outside of the physical method we know today. They were actual, physical experiences.

Q. If you knew that Jesus could be contacted any-where, why did you go to India to unearth these truths?

A. We did not go there for that purpose.

Q. Have you personally ever transported your physi-cal or astral body?

A. I know nothing about the astral body. We have had our physical bodies transported many times. We have never been able to determine how it came about but the very fact that it was brought about is proof that it can be accomplished again. It is only a matter of going about it in the right way.

Q. Does lack of forgiveness limit the power of our love?

138

A. There is no limit to love or forgiveness or principle. We can use them in every direction for every condition. Just let go of the condition and revert back to principle. The moment we have forgiven we are right back to principle.

CHAPTER XI

MEN WHO WALKED WITH THE MASTER

I THINK many of you have planted seeds or set out plants and loved them and watched them grow. Plants will respond very readily. Luther Burbank never sent out a plant from his garden unless it responded to his voice. George Washington Carver did the same thing. I worked with George Washington Carver and I knew Luther Burbank from the time he was six years old.

Luther Burbank always said, and it disturbed his mother and father very much because they did not understand it, that Jesus worked with him all the time.

One Sunday afternoon he walked with his father over to visit a neighbor. They took a short cut through the fields and passed through a potato patch. As children will do, little Luther Burbank ran ahead. It was at the time when the potato blooms were ripening. One stem was standing up a little higher than all the others and Luther stopped to look at it, and his father said when he came up that the flower was waving back and forth and the boy said to him, "Papa, that's talking to me." "Well," the father told my father, "I thought the boy was going wrong and I hurried him on and went over to the neighbor's." All the time they were there Luther

141

was anxious to return, and finally, about half past three they started homeward. They returned through the same potato field, the boy rushing ahead and going directly to this same plant. There was a great calm over the field, not a leaf moved. When the father came up to where the boy was standing, that tall seed pod was moving again, back and forth, and Luther said, "Papa, I want to stay here. Jesus is talking to me and telling me what to do." His father took him home and made him do his chores and sent him to bed. In a short time he found him stealing downstairs trying to get out of the house. He was sent back to bed three different times that night. By that time it was eleven o'clock and the parents thought the boy was asleep for the night.

The next morning Luther was missing. The father walked out into the field and there he found the boy wrapped around that potato hill just as close as he could get to it, sound asleep. When he was awakened he said, "Papa, Jesus talked with me all night long and He told me that if I would watch that little bulb until it ripened, take it and preserve it and plant the seed next Spring, that when it developed there would be one potato there that would make me famous," — and that is just what happened!

Luther Burbank also worked with the cactus. He took the prickly pear and put it into a glass cage where it would be protected. For five and a half months he sat before that case one hour each day and talked to that prickly pear something like this: "Now you are protected, you don't need those spikes, let them go." In seven and a half months the spikes had dropped off. He had the spikeless cactus.

Luther Burbank used to say: "Why, I walk and talk with Jesus, and He with me. He teaches me! He tells me what to do."

****

F. L. Rawson was a brother of Sir Rawson-Rawson, one of the great engineers of England. He was called in by the *Daily Mail* to investigate Christian Science and he did such a remarkable work that they were all astonished. His first statement was, "There is nothing but God in God's perfect world. Man is the image, the likeness, passing on God's ideas to his fellow man with perfect regularity and ease."

One day when I was visiting Mr. Rawson in London we stood at a window looking out across the street. In London years ago they used two-wheel carts drawn by one horse. Construction work was in progress across the way and a horse pulling a two-wheeled cart came down the street, halted, backed up, the driver went to the back of the cart, and suddenly, before the eye could catch what happened, the box turned up and tipped the whole load of rock right on him. F. L. Rawson's statement was, "There is nothing but God," and that man seemed to come right up through the rocks, and he didn't have a scratch on him.

Another thing happened in that same connection. The horse didn't do something that suited him and the owner started to beat the horse. All Mr. Rawson did was to tap on the window to attract the man's attention. That horse immediately walked over and put his nose up against the window!

F. L. Rawson took one hundred men into World War I and came out without a scratch on any of them, and they went through some of the most rugged assignments. He stood absolutely for that statement: *"There is nothing but God."*

****

We can go on and state almost indefinitely what happens as we take the right attitude toward a thing. Now we know that, if we stand off and look at a thing and say that is impossible, the very next thing you know somebody else will come along and complete that in a short time. That has been so with practically everything.

Alexander Graham Bell was a good example. Our family knew him very well. He lived in Jamestown, New York. He walked sixty miles from Jamestown to Buffalo, New York to contact my father and his two brothers, who were small bankers in Buffalo at the time, and asked them to let him have two thousand dollars that he might attend Boston Tech to perfect his instrument and install it in the Centennial grounds in Philadelphia in 1876. They let him have the money. When the directors of the bank learned of the loan they came to my father and uncles and asked for their resignation, they were so sure Bell would never perfect his telephone. Booths were installed at the Centennial, people could pay a nickel, go into those booths and call up and talk to their friends in another booth, and that little device created such interest that it paid more money than anything that was installed at the Centennial Exposition.

You see, we close our thoughts and we lose the benefit of them.

Alexander Graham Bell was really a wonderful character. The reason he didn't have any money was because he was always helping the blind. He spent every bit of money he had to aid the blind.

****

Dr. Norwood used to tell his little congregation that he would go for a walk out among the timber in back of the church and there Jesus would join him and they would walk on and on together.

Dr. Norwood had a small church up in Nova Scotia at a little place where there were only twenty-nine fishermen and their families in the village. Somehow, word of this got out and we heard of it and went up there with the idea of taking photographs. We took the pictures on a Bell & Howell camera with the ordinary lens and we have those pictures today.

Some time later Dr. Norwood was called to Saint Bartholomew's Church in New York City and in less than five months that church was so crowded that they had to put loud speakers outside that all who came might hear him.

One Christmas season during a healing service hour at the church, Jesus was seen to walk out from behind the altar and pass right down the main aisle of the church. I talked to over 500 of the people who

145

were gathered there and saw this happen and Jesus' salutation was: "Prepare to put love forth to the whole universe."

****

The Chelas in India have a very beautiful prayer which you will note is not a beseeching prayer:

"I go forth this day in all things immersed wholly in God and God's abundance. The conquering Christ stands forth one with God's abundance and in every activity of this day. Now I know that I am God's supreme child. I move each moment of this day immersed in God and God's divine love. God! God! God! The great flame of love flows through every atom of my whole being. I Am the pure golden flame of God. I pour this divine flame through my physical body. The conquering Christ salutes you, God, my Father. Peace! Peace! Peace! The great peace of God prevails!"

CHAPTER XII

CREDO

*T*HE GOAL is God. You can start your day with God by taking your first thought of God within your own form. Let me say that the goal is established and always has been established. You are divine. The Divine Image, God, the Christ of God. God men. God women.

Let me also state that there is no thing or no one to compel you to think of these things. It must be a free will offering to your God-self:

God I Am united with universal life and power, and all of this strength is focused in my entire nature, making me so positive with God perfect energy that I send it out to every form, and I make it so positive that all may be transformed into harmony and perfection. I know that they are all in accord with infinite life and God freedom and peace.

My mind is fully polarized with Infinite Intelligent Wisdom. Every faculty of my entire body finds free expression through my mind and all humanity does express the same.

My heart is filled to overflowing with peace, love, and joy of the conquering Christ. I see in every face that conquering Christ. My heart is strong with God love and I know that it fills the heart of all humanity. God life fully enriches my entire blood stream and fills my body with the purity of Divine Life.

God is all life. I am inspired with life with every breath and my lungs take in life with every breath and it fills my blood stream with vitalizing life.

God my stomach is the digestive energy of intelligent and almighty life. Every organ of my body is infused with health and harmony and my entire organism works in complete harmony.

I know that all of my organs are infused with God intelligence. All are conscious of their duties and they work together for the health and harmony of my entire being.

God I Am the energy that fills all space. I am constantly drawing in this energy from all-pervading God life. I know that God is that all-wise and loving intelligence imparting to me the mighty God life and I realize the full dominion from God, the Indwelling Presence in my complete body form.

I praise God within for the healing perfection of life. All is life and I allow all life to come into expression.

The Conquering Christ says, "My words are Spirit and they are life" *and* "If a man keep My words he will never see death."

The intelligent Christ, the Conquering Christ, sends forth abundance of love to the entire universe.

Supreme Mind is everything. I Am Supreme Mind!

I Am Supreme Wisdom, Love, and Power. From the very depth of my heart I shout the glad thanksgiving that I Am this sublime and exhaustless Wisdom and I demand that I draw it to myself and become completely conscious of this ceaseless Wisdom.

Remember that THOUGHTS AND SPOKEN WORDS ARE THINGS!

Shout the glad tidings of joy that you are free, completely free from all limiting conditions. Then KNOW that you are free and go forth triumphantly free!

I AM REBORN INTO THE PERFECT POWER OF THE SUPREME MIND OF GOD. GOD I AM.

Let us walk among all people with the full realization that we exist to impart the joyous Light of Love to every soul. This is in reality the greatest privilege. For as we radiate that boundless love of God to every soul, our souls thrill with the Holy Spirit; we also feel the love of God for all humanity. To feel and know this is to feel and know the Conquering Christ in all humanity. This endows us with the healing power and wisdom that Jesus is endowed with.

During his lectures the last two years of his life, Baird Spalding often recited the words of a poem written by John Gillespie Magee, Jr., a Royal Canadian Air Force pilot who was shot down over England on December 11, 1941, at the age of nineteen.

Shortly before his death, John Magee sent his mother the poem, High Flight, which was soon to become known the world over and is still considered the greatest poem to come out of World War II.

Because it was his favorite verse, we feel Mr. Spalding would like the words of High Flight included in this volume. (Editor)

HIGH FLIGHT

Oh, I have slipped the surly bonds of Earth
And danced the skies on laughter-silvered wings.
Sunward I've climbed, and joined the
    tumbling mirth
Of sun-split clouds, — and done a hundred things
You have not dreamed of — wheeled and soared
    and swung
High in the sunlit silence. Hov'ring there,
I've chased the shouting wind along, and flung
My eager craft through footless halls of air . . .

Up, up the long, delirious, burning blue
I've topped the wind-swept heights with easy grace,
Where never lark, or even eagle flew —
And, while with silent, lifting mind I've trod
The high, untrespassed sanctity of space,
Put out my hand and touched the face of God.

For a Complete Price List of
Inspirational, Self-help & Metaphysical Books,
write to:

DeVorss & Co., *Publishers*
P. O. Box 550
Marina del Rey, Calif. 90294